D0021073

THE GEORGE GUND FOUNDATION
IMPRINT IN AFRICAN AMERICAN STUDIES

The George Gund Foundation has endowed this imprint to advance understanding of the history, culture, and current issues of African Americans.

miles and me

Quincy Troupe

miles and me

University of California Press
Berkeley Los Angeles London

An earlier version of the section entitled "The *Spin* Interview" in Chapter 1 first appeared in *Conjunctions* 16 (1991).

University of California Press
Berkeley and Los Angeles, California

University of California Press, Ltd.
London, England

Library of Congress
Cataloging-in-Publication Data

Troupe, Quincy.
Miles and me / Quincy Troupe.
p. cm.
Includes index.
ISBN 0-520-21624-5 (cloth : alk. paper)
1. Davis, Miles. 2. Jazz musicians—United States—Biography. 3. Troupe, Quincy.
I. Title.

ML419.D39 T76 2000
788.92'165'092—dc21
[B] 99-054370

Manufactured in the United States of America
08 07 06 05 04 03 02 01 00
10 9 8 7 6 5 4 3 2

The paper used in this publication meets the minimum requirements of ANSI/NISO Z39.48-1992 (R 1997) (*Permanence of Paper*).⊗

contents

prologue

Miles Davis was a great poet on his instrument. His horn could blow warm, round notes that spoke to the deepest human emotions, and it could spit out cracked trills that evoked the angry sounds of bullets firing. Sometimes his trumpet seemed to float over and through remarkably complex rhythms and time signatures with heart-stopping speed and efficiency. His sound could penetrate like a sharp knife. It could also be muted, tender and low, like a lullaby, but it was always charged with deeply felt emotion. Miles' sound always made us sit up and take notice. It was burnished, brooding, unforgettable.

When you heard Miles on the radio, you knew right away that it was him. You knew it *by* the sound because no one else ever sounded like that. Like Louis Armstrong's, Duke Ellington's, Thelonious Monk's, John Coltrane's, his voice was unmistakably unique.

Sometimes when he used the mute, whether on up-tempo tunes or slow ones, we knew we were hearing perfection. When he played muted ballads, it was as if he were tenderly kissing our feelings—then he would stun us with bright, rapid-fire bursts of notes that penetrated our souls. Miles not only soliloquized, he also had a "dialoging" style. It was like listening to him having a conversation with himself, with one of his voices imitating a fast-talking, sweet-rapping black street hustler.

Even when he was first starting out, Miles' sound and style got your attention immediately, because you knew whatever he played, it was going to be unusual. His music was always unusual because that's the way his mind worked—unusually. Miles Davis was *always* unusual. He didn't get that way just after he became famous—he was special from the beginning.

His homeboys back in East St. Louis understood that. They knew that he was odd, a little bit different from them and everyone else. They didn't mind his eccentricities. They gave him the space to be different all his life—but only as long as he didn't step over the invisible line that both he and they knew was there. Miles seldom crossed that line to "diss" them, because if he had, those homeboys would have made him pay. They weren't no "pootbutts."

Miles knew, too, that they understood him in the way that homeboys always understand the one among them who is different. Odd. A genius. Someone who sees things they never see. Hears sounds they never hear. Voices. The screech of car tires. Maybe a mockingbird riffing on another bird's song. The lonely voice of an old black churchwoman singing plaintively in the dusky glow of a backwater country evening, somewhere few come to, save mosquitoes or rats or evil white men dressed in bedsheets, carrying guns and flaming crosses.

In the night air, the trains never seem to stop whistling past, their wheels humming. The roads are unpaved, empty, eerie in the twilight just before the hants come out to enter everybody's imagination and shut down those dusty roads. The voice of the old black woman floats above the shadows and trees, disembodied yet whole. It rides up there and cruises alongside the night birds circling above some unseen church or log cabin, in some out-of-the-way location back in the bushes, hidden. The voice also circles. Plaintive. Haunting. Achingly real.

And if you had the privilege of hearing that voice, perhaps you wouldn't file it away as anything special, something to imitate and relate to for the rest of your life—a reference point for your own life's experiences, making you sensitive, alert, cognizant of other beautiful, necessary things. But that's the way Miles heard it.

Perhaps the voice would remind you of a lonely trumpet sound. But maybe you wouldn't know that what you heard was special because you couldn't see that old black woman's face. And, if you could have met her, you might have been too busy watching her chaw on some snuff to see the wisdom in her old eyes. But Miles did see that face, saw it when he heard her voice. He saw the whole scene, took it all in. Knew that it was real and special and filed it away for later use.

From the "giddyap," Miles' friends knew he saw and heard

things they could never see or hear. They told me so. And so they protected him. He was allowed to be and do whatever was necessary for him as long as he was cool and didn't disrespect them by looking down on them.

He never stuck his nose all up in the wind as if he smelled something foul when his homeboys walked into a room. No. He never treated them that way. Even when he was looking down from the elevated heights they had helped him to climb, he never cultivated an attitude that would have angered or hurt them. He was always just "one of the boys," even if they knew—and he knew—he was also apart from them.

His fame never got in the way. His East St. Louis homeboys were his best friends up to the day he died. He trusted and knew them and they trusted and knew him. To them he was always "Little Davis," or "Junior," or "Dewey," or "Buckwheat"—a name he hated because it alluded to the blackness of his skin, which he was sensitive about all of his life. But some of his old friends called him that anyway, despite his protests, because that's what they had called him back in East St. Louis when they were all young and full of piss and vinegar and thrived on insulting each other, to see who was the strongest.

St. Louis and East St. Louis were—and still are—great trumpet towns. That's because there were so many marching drum and bugle corps bands, which were part of a tradition brought over to St. Louis by Germans from their fatherland—although I don't ever recall seeing a white drum and bugle corps marching band. (That's not to say there weren't any; I just never saw one.) But it was the black marching bands in St. Louis and East St. Louis who put their distinctive creative stamp on the tradition—the high-stepping kicks and the swaying back and forth of the bugles as they were played were black innovations—and who raised the practice almost to a high art form.

Based in individual black communities and sponsored by local African-American chapters of the Elks and various Masonic orders, these marching bands would liven up the streets on weekends during the spring, summer, and early fall, and I remember them with great fondness. I looked forward with anticipation whenever word came down that they would be gracing my St. Louis neighborhood with their sounds and presence.

These bands developed a style of playing the bugle, later transferred to the cornet and trumpet, that became known as the St. Louis "running" style. Pioneered by Eddie Randall, Levi Madison, Harold "Shorty" Baker, and Clark Terry (Miles' real first mentor in trumpet style) and perfected by Miles (who, in his youth, had played in several East St. Louis marching bands), it was characterized by musical ideas, chords, and notes strung together in a continuous blowing, dialoging manner, akin to a fast-talking conversationalist. (Trumpeter Lester Bowie, from St. Louis, provides an example of this style today.)

This distinctive St. Louis sound was connected to the great trumpet tradition of New Orleans by the musicians who traveled on the riverboats shuttling up and down the Mississippi. But where New Orleans trumpet players employed a hotter, bigger, brassier style (as exemplified by Buddy Bolden, Freddie Keppard,

Louis Armstrong, Al Hirt, Wynton Marsalis, Nicholas Payton, and Terrence Blanchard), the St. Louis style was generally cooler, more subtle and conversational (although it, too, could be hot and brassy at times).

The different styles came out of different cultures. New Orleans is a lively city with a coastal culture heavily influenced by the French, Spanish, Native American, and African peoples. With its Mardi Gras, Congo Square, African ring dance, Voodoo Queen Marie Laveau, African drumming, Cajun fiddling, and Creole cooking, the culture of the Crescent City is thoroughly intermingled like a great big pot of gumbo or jambalaya.

St. Louis, on the other hand, is a city founded by the French but controlled by Germans. And although many other ethnic groups (French, Italians, Jews, Hungarians, Native Americans, and African Americans) have had an impact, the culture is pervasively German. It is more Calvinistic than Catholic, more marching band than Mardi Gras. It is a culture where a show of emotion is considered uncouth, almost uncivilized. Thus, a much more restrained musical culture developed among St. Louis blacks, one that took a much cooler approach. The one citywide parade, the Veil Prophet Parade, was for nearly one hundred years a whites-only event. (The parade and ball were finally integrated in the 1970s.) Such parades were sedate, dull affairs. I witnessed many and never saw anyone dance with any saints or speak to any spirits. Blacks had the Annie Malone Parade to get by on, but even this was no joyous, celebratory affair; rather, it was cool and laid back. If New Orleans is gumbo and jambalaya,

St. Louis is chitterlings, barbecue, mashed potatoes and gravy. That Miles grew up in this cooler musical milieu is reflected in his approach to music and in the man himself.

It is only fitting, then, that the story of my relationship with Miles begins in St. Louis, where I first heard him play. This book describes how his music and personality affected my life and the lives of a generation who looked for proud, "unreconstructed" black men to admire and emulate. It also examines, through the lens of Miles' life, how it is that jazz, this country's classical music, is always neglected—until it conforms to the white majority's expectations—because it is perceived as a black art form. The genius of Miles Davis is in many ways the genius of jazz, a genius that is often overlooked, to the great loss of American culture.

One note about the possessive spelling of Miles' name in this book. I write "Miles'" without the extra "s" because that is how I hear it. Without the apostrophe and added "s," his name sounds right to me, open-mouthed and familiar. I know that traditionally only a few great names that end in "s"—like Jesus' and Moses'—have been spelled this way. I trust that my breaking with this tradition and placing Miles' name in such illustrious company will not offend anyone. Miles Davis was first and foremost all about sound, and so am I.

one

meeting miles

I first met Miles Davis in 1978 or so at a party at a Dr. Leo Maitland's. Leo, who had at one time been one of Miles' doctors, lived down the hall from me at 382 Central Park West and had become a very good friend. I had been listening to Miles since 1954 and he had been a hero to me for a long time. But by 1978 I wasn't listening to his records as much as I had earlier in my life, although I still loved going to hear him play live.

Before I actually met Miles at Leo's, I had seen him a couple of times in the elevator of my building because he lived in the same neighborhood and was dating one of my former poetry workshop students. Yvonne or Evette Duret—they were identical twins, so I can't remember which one, but I think it was Evette who lived in the same building I did. I had also caught glimpses of him a few times at neighborhood bars. He would sit in a corner hidden behind his ever-present dark glasses looking menacingly at everyone. Sometimes I spotted him at after-hours joints. Other times I saw him hurrying through the neighborhood streets, walking or driving his red Ferrari sports coupe.

Like I said, we lived in the same neighborhood, the Upper West Side of Manhattan. But whenever we passed each other, no matter where it was, I was never tempted to say even a mumbling word to him. That was because I had a very clear memory of how angry he could become at unwanted public attention. The memory was more than twenty years old but was still as vivid to me as though the scene had happened the day before yesterday.

peacock alley

It was July of 1956 and I had just seen my idol, Miles Davis, in person, for the first time. He was playing at St. Louis's premier jazz spot, Peacock Alley, in downtown St. Louis. I had been able to get in because I had a false draft card that said I was over twenty-one, though I was only seventeen.

I remember how "sharp" and "clean" Miles looked, and how he seemed so totally in control. He was completely mesmerizing. He was everything I thought he would be. Fascinated by the man's presence, I watched his every move, as did everybody else in the club.

Miles' music was sensational that night. The band he brought with him included a great surprise: instead of Sonny Rollins, who'd been advertised, he brought John Coltrane. My friends and I were all big Sonny Rollins fans, so we were very disappointed when he didn't show. John Coltrane? Who was he? We soon found out. Trane just blew everybody's mind. Miles was grinning like a Cheshire cat because he knew people would be disappointed Sonny Rollins hadn't shown. His grin and his attitude seemed to say, "but how could y'all ever doubt me? How could y'all think I would ever have brought somebody bad to my hometown for y'all to hear?" Paul Chambers, Philly Joe Jones, and Red Garland were also in the band and they were great, but the night belonged to Trane and Miles. When we left the club, their names were on everyone's lips.

That was also the night of the incident that left me with an indelible memory of Miles' temper. The way it happened was like this: Among the St. Louis "in crowd" everyone and his mama knew not to walk up to Miles if you didn't know him and just start talking to him like he was your long-lost friend. It didn't matter whether you were hip and black or hip and white. If you didn't know Miles, you didn't approach him.

My friends and I were part of the younger "in crowd," and the word had come down from older hip guys—like my cousin Marvin—that if you did walk up to Miles and try to talk to him, he just might bite your head off with a real cold-blooded cussin' out. So the thing to do was just to lay back and watch him from afar, like he was some kind of untouchable piece of fine jewelry around some fine woman's neck and, in a weird sort of way, I guess that's what Miles was like—a rare gem.

Anyway, that's what everyone was doing when the group took a break—we were all watching Miles from a distance. Then, all of a sudden, this voice from somewhere behind us said, "Oh look, darling, there's Miles Davis. Let's go up and say hello!"

We all turned around, amazed to see this young white couple walking earnestly through the crowd with these innocent looks of expectation on their faces. They made a beeline straight for Miles, who was standing at the bar drinking a beer, smoking a cigarette, and surveying everyone around him disdainfully from behind those dark sunglasses. I remember looking at the friends who had come with me that evening—Fred Arnold, Leonard Anderson, Percy Campbell, and my cousin Donald Troupe—and laughing nervously under my breath in anticipation of what was going to happen. Everybody else in the bar was watching with keen interest, too. That whole roomful of people was holding its collective breath in anticipation of how Miles was going to respond.

When the young couple got close to Miles, the man stuck out his right hand in anticipation of a handshake and said, "How you doing Miles, my name is—"

He didn't even manage to get his name out before Miles, with cold-blooded, biting fury in his voice, spat out, "Fuck you, you jive punk-ass motherfucka! Get the fuck outta my face and take yo silly little bitch with you!"

The words were fired like bullets, and they penetrated the young man's heart. A stunned look spread across his face. I felt kind of sorry for him. I watched complete embarrassment spread like a scarlet wave over the man and woman's white faces. They were rendered totally speechless by the deep freeze of Miles' words.

Then, having stopped the couple dead in their tracks with his harsh and scornful attitude, Miles simply turned his back on them like the king he was in his own mind. (And in everybody else's mind that night, too.) He took a long drag off his cigarette and blew a jet of smoke toward the ceiling. Then he took a long deep swallow of beer. He dismissed the young couple just like they weren't even there. *It was something.*

I had never seen a white man treated like that by a black man. And although I did feel a little sorry for the couple, deep down it made me feel really good because white people have always believed that they can walk up to any black person, and no matter where we are or what we are doing, say any and everything to us, no matter how silly and ignorant it might be. Most white people think that just because they're white and privileged and we're black that we're at their beck and call, that they can get away saying anything to anyone who's not white. Maybe that's the way they think it's going to be, forever.

But that night Miles showed everybody in that club that he wasn't about to take shit from anyone, black or white. (I, for one, after that night, absorbed that lesson and adopted a similar attitude, although my stance could never be as dismissive as Miles' was. Ever.)

As the young couple walked away with their heads hung low, I remember thinking how cruel and heartless Miles' actions seemed. But I also remember thinking that what I had witnessed was consistent with what I had heard about his character. Having bought into his legend, I would have expected him to do just what he did. Anything less would not have met my expectations of what Miles was really like.

After all, who did that young white guy think he was, going up to Miles like that? Hadn't he heard the stories? Did he really think Miles was going to talk to him?

To tell the truth, I really didn't feel that much pity for the couple. Maybe I felt that Miles was doing to some white person what I had always wished I could do because of how it was for black people in this country: we were oppressed, despised, our spirits beaten down—in many cases, killed—by a callous white majority. So whatever pity I felt for the couple was minimal.

I didn't totally understand Miles' harsh treatment of that couple that evening but I did learn one thing. *I never wanted to see myself in that situation.* Later, when I got to know him personally, I would find out that Miles dealt with most people in this harsh manner—whether they were black, white, or whatever—whenever they invaded his privacy. He felt he had to be that way just to keep people off of him because of his shyness.

Miles believed that if he had a reputation for dealing with strangers brutally when they approached him in public, then they should do so with the full knowledge that they might have their hearts, heads, and egos served up to them on a platter. He told me this many times, and I watched him inflict this kind of punishment on people time and time again.

The memory of Miles cussing out that white couple influenced the way I felt about the man ever after. That image of him—impervious and imperial, standing "clean as a broke-dick dog" at the bar in Peacock Alley, coolly drinking and smoking a cigarette—is forever carved into my consciousness like a stone engraving. I especially didn't want Miles to ever cuss me out the way he did that white couple because I didn't know how I would respond. So I kept my respectful distance from the man. But the night at Leo's would change all that, and after many years of admiring him from afar, I would finally find myself up close, sitting right next to him.

leo's party

When I arrived at Leo's party the only seat left open was right next to Miles, who was dressed, as he usually was back in those days, all in black. I guess no one wanted to brave sitting next to him and I didn't either, really, but there was no other place to sit down. I was surprised to see him there, tearing away at the food on his plate. Even while eating, he managed to maintain that menacing "don't-fuck-with-me" aura he always seemed to carry around as part of his persona. I got some food and sat down next to him. He looked at me, kind of surprised that someone was bold enough to enter his space. Then I heard him say in that famous scratchy voice of his, "What's happenin'?"

"Nothin'," I said without even looking at him, afraid he might scorch me with his eyes, even from behind his dark shades.

"Oh, yeah?" he said, looking sideways at me, a sardonic grin playing at the corners of his lips, which were greasy and shiny with what he was eating.

"You sure of that?" he added, looking back down at his food.

"Sure of what?" I asked, a little confused.

"That nothin' is happenin' here. You sure of that?"

"No, I'm not sure that nothin's happenin'. Maybe it is but I don't see it."

"Well," he said, looking directly at me. "You see that fine motherfuckin' bitch standing over there, don't you? You gonna tell me she ain't what's goin' on?"

I looked at the woman he was nodding toward—tall, brown-skinned, slim, and well-built, with a dancer's body—and said without hesitation, "Yeah, I see what you mean. She is happenin'."

"Tell me about it!" he said, nodding his head. "Man, that woman's fine-na than a motherfucka."

"You got that right," I said, nodding my head in approval. "Yeah, you sho-nuff got that right."

"You a musician?" he said, looking at me curiously, chewing hard on his food, then looking back down at his plate.

"No, I'm a poet," I told him.

"No shit?" he said, looking at me again, but harder this time, holding my face in the twin dark mirrors of his shades before going back to his food.

"A poet. No shit."

Then he didn't say another word. When he got up to leave about fifteen minutes later, he looked at me, shook my hand, and said, "Later."

That was it. He was gone, out the door, into the night air of Manhattan like a figment of my wildest imagination.

I sensed the boxer in Miles that evening—something he had once desperately wanted to be—an edginess that clearly came across in his music.

on the street

The next time I saw Miles was about two weeks later. He was walking down Broadway between 81st and 82d Streets coming toward me, on the west side of the street, dressed all in black again, including a black hat and dark shades. From a distance I watched his mouth furiously working over some chewing gum, his jaws grinding like pistons.

He was in a hurry and was moving rapidly toward me, head up, expression fierce, with that hip, hip-dedip strut and glide, that bouncy walk with a dip in the middle that was his gait. His signature "no-nonsense," cool musician's strut that I got to know so well much later. He was looking straight ahead, not noticing anyone or anything but focused on some imaginary place he held fixed in his head.

Some people were looking at him as they passed by, and some even whispered, "That's Miles Davis," but nobody had the courage to stop or say "Hello." Not even a "Hey, Miles." The space that existed around him and locked him in was weird. He was like a king, or at least a prince. His moniker was "The Prince of Darkness," but I would add "The Prince of Light"—because of his magical trumpet playing, yes sir, he was the cock-of-the-walk rooster bringing the light out of the darkness.

And that day all of us out there on the street with him were his subjects. We couldn't even come close to touching him, though he was walking alone, without bodyguards. No crown, save his attitude. But, then, his attitude was enough. He had no need for bodyguards or a visible crown to let us know he was royalty because we all knew he was, and because he was his own best protection. His take-no-prisoners attitude surrounded him like a suit of steel armor.

It was a little past midday and a warm sun was smiling down and smoothing out my vibe. Because I had met him just a couple of weeks back at Leo's party, and because he had talked to me, I thought he would remember who I was. So, when he was a few feet in front of me, I smiled in anticipation, lifted my hand in greeting, and said, "Hey, how ya doin', Miles?"

He didn't blink or break stride but blew right on by just as if I wasn't even there. Didn't say a word. Nothing. Nothing but intense energy moving through space. Later, I would hear him liken himself to a tornado wind—a force of nature. Was his energy dark or light that day? I was so transfixed I couldn't tell. He didn't slow down or hesitate or anything; he just kept right on steppin'. Moving away.

I was shocked. Stunned, but not rendered mute. So I called out his name again as the distance between us grew, "Hey, Miles, it's me, Quincy Troupe, the poet. I met you over at Leo Maitland's."

I said this to his back. But he didn't even pause, not to mention look around. Just kept right on steppin'. And before I knew it, he had hooked a left and disappeared around the corner of 82d Street. When he turned that corner I felt really humiliated, the smile wiped off my face.

Feeling exposed and foolish, I looked around sheepishly to see if anyone had noticed. A few people seemed to be snickering at me under their smug smiles. I turned around and walked down Broadway, head down, ego shaken, feeling puzzled and angry.

"Why would he treat me like that?" I asked myself rhetorically, even though I already knew the answer. My cousin Marvin (now deceased) had told me the answer long ago, the first time I ever saw Miles up close and in person back in St. Louis's Peacock Alley. "Don't speak to Miles," Marvin had said, just before Miles had humiliated that white boy for daring to speak to him. "Miles don't like people coming up and talking to him unless he knows them real good."

Marvin had told me not to speak to Miles, and he was right. I knew this. I had felt Miles' dark energy in those bars and after-hours joints. But hardheaded me—with plenty of ego to spare—I had to learn, the hard way, that I didn't know Miles Davis at all, even though I may have thought I did after talking to him at Leo's. Clearly, as far as Miles was concerned, that meeting didn't even come close to qualifying me as an acquaintance, even though inside my own head, I had thought it did.

I ran into Miles a couple of months later, again at a party thrown by Leo. Out of anger—or curiosity, or stupidity—I walked right up to him while he was eating a plate of fish and asked him why he had "shined me on so bad" that day out on Broadway. He was alone and, without missing a beat, he fixed me with one of those fierce, almost evil looks—a look I saw many, many times later after I got to know him well—and said, "Fuck you, man! I don't hafta speak to your motherfuckin' ass every time I see you. Shit, who the fuck you think you are?"

And with that said, he went back to finishing his food.

I didn't say anything, which shocked me, because normally I'm not the quiet type who lets anybody get away with talking to me that way. Normally I would have said a nasty "Fuck you" back. Maybe I would even have gone upside the person's head for disrespecting me. But I didn't say anything, much less go upside his head. I just looked at him—probably with a hurt expression on my face—and stayed silent, stunned by his ferocity.

I was also still suffering from a bad case of hero worship, which more than likely had something to do with rendering me mute. Again. The good thing was that only a few people heard how he talked to me that night, not everybody who was there. But those who had heard looked at me with that smug air of disapproval that people assume when someone as famous as Miles "screams on" someone else less famous.

Like, you know, it all had to be my fault. It couldn't have been his, so why didn't I just sit my ass down and enjoy being in the man's presence—without trying to say a word or really interact with him—the way everyone else was doing? But I was so embarrassed, again. He didn't say another word to me for the rest of the time he was there. But from time to time, I would catch him looking hard and evil at me, and I can tell you, those looks sent shivers up and down my spine. Before I knew it, he was gone again, had slipped out into the night without any fanfare. Like one of his mysterious solos, he was there and then suddenly gone, a wisp of smoke into the night.

the dark years

After that I didn't speak to Miles for several years. From time to time I would see him sliding around in the darkness of bars and after-hours joints, a drink and cigarette in his hands, dark shades on, usually all in black, whispering into the ears of fine ladies, or huddled with some very suspicious-looking street hustlers.

I ran into him in the elevator of my building again. We were alone, standing side by side, but his cold demeanor warned me not to greet him, and I didn't. By then I had learned my lesson well. (I remember wondering, though, if this was the way he whipped the musicians in his band into line—by intimidating them?) When he reached his floor, he got off the elevator without acknowledging me. After he left I could still feel the power of the man, the force of his demonic spirit and personality. I was almost happy to see him go.

But it was this same demonic force that propelled his music into magical, powerful, mysterious genius. Whatever I felt about the man, one thing I had learned was certain: up close and personal there was no denying that he possessed an impressive, powerful presence, and whether you liked it or not, he channeled this power into his ever-changing music.

From time to time during the dark years from 1975 to 1980, when Miles was away from music, when he wasn't even practicing, stories about his sexual orgies, his excessive use of cocaine and alcohol, and his reclusive craziness would drift through the conversations I overheard at bars and parties.

Many of these stories are as comical as they are pathetic. For instance, there was the time when Miles abandoned his Ferrari in the middle of West End Avenue after spotting a policeman he thought was following him. He was so paranoid and high on cocaine that he ran into an apartment building and jumped into an elevator. A startled white woman was already inside the elevator, and when he saw her, he slapped her face and asked her what she was doing in his car. She ran screaming out of the elevator and Miles took it up to the top floor, where he stayed, hiding in the garbage disposal room until late in the evening.

When I would ask my friend Leo about Miles, he would just shake his head and tell me he couldn't comment on what was happening because of doctor-patient confidentiality. But by the look in Leo's eyes, I could tell that what was going on with Miles was not good.

the comeback

Fortunately for Miles—and for music—that grim period didn't last too many years. In early 1980 word began to creep out that

Miles was back in the studio recording. This announcement created a tremendous amount of excitement. There was talk of concerts. Miles' eagerly awaited comeback album, *The Man with a Horn,* was released later that year. Early in the summer of 1981, Miles played live at a small club called Kix in Cambridge, Massachusetts. Then it was announced that he would be appearing at the 1981 Newport Kool Jazz Festival in New York City. The excitement around this concert reached a fever pitch so quickly that all the tickets were sold in the blink of an eye. And on a hot July night that year, Miles played to a screaming, cheering, standing-room-only audience at Avery Fisher Hall. That concert (along with some music from the Kix engagement and some concerts Miles played later that summer in Japan) is preserved on Columbia's live recording *We Want Miles,* which was released in the fall of 1981. *Star People* was released in 1982, around the time that Miles married actress Cicely Tyson at Bill Cosby's Massachusetts home. *Decoy* was released in 1984 and *You're Under Arrest* in 1985. That was when I met Miles for the third time. Only this time I was on assignment to write an article about him for *Spin* magazine.

My interview with Miles had been arranged by a former student of mine from Richmond College, Sandra Trim-DaCosta, who had become the head of publicity for Columbia Records' jazz division. She set up the interview and arranged to meet me at Miles' apartment, stressing that I had to get the interview done in an hour and a half.

the *spin* interview

When I left my top-floor apartment on 101st Street and West End Avenue that June day in 1985, it was bright and sunny. As I walked, the tunes of *You're Under Arrest* were threading through my head. (I thought I would base my interview on this, his latest, album since I would have only an hour and a half to do it in.) I had loved the first cut, "One Phone Call / Street Scene," with Miles running down a litany of reasons why black folks get busted and arrested in this country—and for that matter, all over the world—with voice-overs in French and Spanish. I had also loved the hip beat and rhythms of the entire track and, of course, Miles' trumpet.

It was such a great day that I decided to walk through Central Park to get to Miles' place. It was a beautiful day, a blessed day, the kind of day that the Big Apple's political leaders use to advertise New York as America's capital of the arts and center of the financial world. The ads are meant to convince people that the city is a wonderful place to move to and live in.

It was a clear, blue afternoon with a lovely, soft, playful breeze. A day filled with New York's unsurpassed electric street life: runners and bicyclists racing down all the avenues; picnickers, baseball and soccer games, and lovers lying on the grass in Central Park; lovely women strolling, handsome men sauntering on all the streets. Stylish, hip people everywhere. But halfway to Miles' place, I decided to go back and get my car because I suddenly realized that I might need it later if I decided to go someplace.

When I arrived at Miles' apartment building on 79th Street and

Fifth Avenue, I was announced by a tall, rotund Latino doorman smiling under a huge, drooping handlebar mustache. I took the elevator up to Miles' fourteenth-floor apartment full of fearful anticipation. Would Miles remember me and "scream on" me again? Would he ignore me and put me out of his place if he did remember me, as he had done to that unfortunate *Time* magazine reporter back in the 1960s?

On that well-publicized occasion, Miles had excused himself from the interview after talking to the reporter for about five minutes. When he returned after a short while, the writer had asked about a car horn insistently blowing outside of Miles' 77th Street townhouse. Miles had turned to the man and said icily, "That's the cab I called for you a while ago." That was the time Miles was supposed to be on the cover of *Time* but was replaced by Thelonious Monk. As the elevator rose, I kept asking myself, "How will he react to me?"

When I got off the elevator and knocked on the door, a young African-American man, his valet, opened the door and let me in. It was dark inside despite the light streaming in from windows that offered a spectacular view of Central Park. A big-screen television set was on, running images of soap-opera actors gushing their idiotic lines while they mugged for the camera. The walls were painted a muted gray, as were the floors. The room reminded me of the inside of a cave. Clothes were thrown haphazardly in a corner and both blue and red trumpets rested on their sides on another table. I saw a photo of Gil Evans standing on a table but there were no photographs of Miles Davis anywhere. Not one of the numerous awards he had won could be seen either, nor were any of his gold or platinum records mounted on the walls.

(I would later ask him where he kept all the awards he had won, and he took me to a closet in his Malibu home and showed them to me. They were all dumped into the closet, piled high and collecting dust. "You're only as good as what you're playing today," he would tell me then, "so I can't be thinking about no awards when I need to have my head into my music.")

We turned into an alcove off the kitchen and there, in a patch of light beaming in through a back window, sitting at a table drawing figures of a woman onto a sketch pad, was Miles. He was wearing sunglasses in all this darkness. "In character already," I thought to myself. He was a study in total concentration, his head bent down over his pad; he didn't even look up.

His valet didn't disturb him but just stood there, silent, watching and waiting. I could still see the actors mouthing their lines on the television screen. A clock tick-tocked somewhere. Other than that, silence, except for the furious sound of Miles' pencil moving across his pad.

He was dressed down. There was paint all over his torn black denims and scruffy shirt, paint all over his long, elegant hands and fingers, and paint on his wizened but handsome—almost feminine—face. Tubes of paint were scattered all over the table and on the floor around him. Sheets torn from his pad with half-finished drawings of figures lay crumpled up among the paint tubes. I was really shocked by this total mess, but he didn't seem to be aware of it, like he wasn't aware of my presence yet—at least, he wasn't letting on that he was.

So I just stood there, along with the valet, and watched him drawing feverishly, not saying a word. I was shifting my weight back and forth from my bad left leg (an old basketball knee injury) to my good right one until at last he slowly turned his head toward me. He put down his pencil, took off his glasses, looked at me sideways, kind of slanting his face upwards, and, fixing me with those radar-beacon eyes, said, "Man, you're a funny lookin' motherfucka." Then, squinting through the darkness at my dreadlocked hair, he added, "How'd you get your hair like that?"

I was totally shocked by his response to me. It wasn't what I had expected. His take on my dreads was kind of country—human—like people back home, like people from anywhere, when they're being real and not full of bullshit pretensions. It was an honest reaction, something I'm used to, something I prefer, in fact, but I wasn't expecting anything like it from Miles after my previous encounters with him.

I guess I was expecting him to be harsh and cold, the way he was the last time I saw him. Or hip and cool, the legendary slick man of impeccable style and class, he of the kiss-my-ass attitude, the black Romeo. Or maybe I was expecting the one who had ignored me on the street and had stood beside me in the elevator without saying even one word. The one who had dressed me down for asking why he hadn't acknowledged me. I was expecting that one, not this normal sort of guy squinting up at me and asking me about my hair.

"Sit down," he said, pointing at a chair across the cluttered glass table from him. "What do you want to know?"

I sat down and when I looked closer, I noticed that he was wearing a gold and brown hair weave, crushed on the right side, like he had slept on that side during the night. The weave was speckled all over with red, blue, and gold paint. (Later I would discover that this was the way he looked most of the time when he was at home because he was always painting.)

The weave—and the condition it was in—surprised me because either he hadn't been wearing one the last time I saw him up close or maybe I just hadn't noticed it. His openness also surprised me because I'd heard how he hated journalists and being interviewed, so I'd come prepared to have my head bitten off. His seemingly casual, open attitude threw me off guard—but I warned myself that the interview hadn't even begun yet. I proceeded with caution, the way one negotiates a minefield, and tried not to say or do anything stupid. I started to pull out my list of questions, written on a yellow legal pad, already considering how I would frame the first one.

But before I could get my pad out he reached across the table with his long bony fingers, grabbed a long lock of my dreaded hair, and started rolling it around between the ends of two fingertips, asking if it was "for real." And before I knew what I was doing, I slapped his hand away from my hair and said, controlling my voice as much as possible, "I grew it like this."

He looked at his hand in disbelief. I felt his valet tense up behind me. (Later I would find out that the valet had earned his black belt in karate.) Then Miles looked at me, both fury and puzzlement in his eyes, and said, "Motherfucka, are you crazy?"

"Naw, I ain't crazy," I answered calmly. "But my coming here to do a story on you don't give you the right to invade my personal space."

At that he looked at me kind of funny, still puzzled. He was probably debating whether he should kick me out or not. Then he shrugged it off, a hint of a smile flickered around his lips, and he bent back over his pad and started drawing again. I felt the valet relax.

Miles asked me where I was from.

"St. Louis," I said. "Remember? We met once at Leo Maitland's."

"Oh yeah, I remember you now," he said, looking at me more closely. "You're that crazy motherfuckin' poet I cursed out at Leo's, right?"

"Right," I said, kind of surprised that he remembered.

"Yeah," he rasped, not looking up from his drawing, "you're a crazy motherfucka." Then his face broke out into a broad smile and he said, "Well, motherfucka, just don't sit there, ask me some motherfuckin' questions. What chu want to know, brother?"

And that's how it started. I believe the closeness between us began developing at that precise moment, on Fifth Avenue, in that apartment, and it remained until his death. I don't know for sure because we never talked about it. But it's something I feel deep down in my gut. I think that moment drew me to him and him to me in some strange way. I believe the fact that he liked and respected me had something to do with my slapping his hand away from my hair, something to do with my respect for myself, and my respect for my own space. I believe he related to that because that's the way he was, at all times.

He respected people who would stand up to him. If you couldn't or wouldn't stand up to him, he would—and I was to find this out later—run over you or knock you aside. Miles was always pushing the envelope, testing the parameters, checking the boundaries, both in his art and in his personal relationships. Those who were strong could stick around; those who were weak would run away because they couldn't stand the constant testing, the constant applications of heat and brutal honesty that Miles doled out. To stay around one had to dish it out as well as take it. Every day. He loved and respected you only if you could stay strong.

Another thing that really opened Miles up to me, I think, came up during that same first interview. He told me that the first professional band he had played in back in St. Louis was Eddie Randle's Blue Devils, and I told him that Eddie Randle was a cousin of mine. I remember him smiling at me and saying, "No shit!" Then he launched into a long thing about what a good man Eddie Randle was, what a great band he had had, and how much he had learned while he was in that band—about music, about being a band leader, about life. Throughout all of this, he kept saying,

"No shit? Really, you Eddie's cousin?"

It was true, and after I convinced him with a few well-chosen facts about Eddie—what he looked like, where he lived, that he had been married to an Italian woman for over fifty years, that he owned a very successful funeral home—Miles really opened up to me.

That day I spent ten hours with Miles Davis instead of the hour and a half I had been promised. After Sandra DaCosta arrived and told Miles that the allotted time had passed, he told her he didn't need her "trying to mother him." After three hours had passed she said she had to go and he told her to go ahead, that everything was alright. So she did.

He showed me films of old boxing matches of his heroes Sugar Ray Robinson and Joe Louis, played tapes of his music and a few chords on his electric piano, blew a few trumpet notes for me to illustrate a point, talked to my girlfriend, Margaret, on the telephone, and when she called him "Mr. Davis" came back at her with, "You can call me Miles." He cooked for me and asked if I liked his drawings. When I told him I thought that they were rudimentary but interesting, he said, "Really?" looking at me again in that funny, puzzled way that I would grow so accustomed to later on when I would see something knock him off balance.

Throughout all of this friendliness, I must admit I was struggling fiercely with a sweeping sensation of awe. This is me sitting here next to Miles Davis like this? My idol? Talking with him like we are long lost friends, like equals? It was hard to believe it was happening.

He told me, among other things, about the troubles he was having with George Butler and Wynton Marsalis, and that he was thinking of leaving Columbia for Warner. I was shocked to hear this. He had been with Columbia for so long. But he had decided it was time for him to move on, to get a fresh start with a record company that would allow him to play the kind of rock- and funk-oriented jazz that he was playing in those days, not to mention whatever else was running through his fertile musical imagination. He told me he was looking forward to the move.

"Plus," he said with a grin, "they're gonna give me all the money I need and then some. I'd be a fool *not* to go, you know what I mean?"

Then he started talking about Wynton Marsalis, though it took him a while to get to the point. He started by saying, "People want to know why Eddie Murphy makes so much money. Hell, they hold all the other actors down. So that when one gets loose, that one makes so much money it's a shame."

He paused to collect his thoughts, then continued. "When Bill Cosby won all the awards for best series on television, you could hear a pin drop at the awards ceremony. Because all of those networks outside of NBC had turned his show down. I know because me and Cicely was there. We saw it go down. I think most of them didn't want the show because it was black and positively black. People want to see blacks crawlin' around and Uncle Tommin'. And they like to compare black people who are doin' somethin' with each other. They'll compare Eddie Murphy to Richard Pryor. Compare me with Wynton Marsalis. Not me with Chuck Mangione. But me and Wynton. That's the kind of shit I don't like.

"But if Wynton listens to all that shit," he went on, "they're goin' to fuck him up. I don't be listen' to none of that shit. But he better watch out. They'll make him comfortable and he'll stay right where he is. That's what they want him to be—comfortable. I don't like a person that's comfortable where they are. I like a person that's always movin', changin', one that says, 'What's this? What's that? Why they doin' this?' That's the way Cicely is. And that's the way I am. Been like this all my life."

Warming up to the subject, he went on. "Like, there could be some classical composers instead of a classical soloist like Wynton. Why don't they take some young composers' work and play that instead of all that old shit? I mean, they're gonna have to change sooner or later. Time is gonna make them change. I mean, they gotta stop doin' Tosca and all that dead old classical shit. And Wynton playin' their music. The kind of stuff anybody can do. All you gotta do is practice, practice, practice.

"I told Wynton they should be suckin' his dick for playin' that simple music. I told him I wouldn't bow down to play that music, that they should be glad that someone as talented as Wynton is playing that tired shit. I wouldn't. I did it once, but I wouldn't do it no more.

"I mean, Wynton takin' time off from playin' his own shit to play their shit. And, if he misses one goddamn note, they gonna be on his ass. Naw," he went on, shaking his head, "I don't think no honor should be bestowed on a black person just 'cause he's playin' some fuckin' 'Flight of the Bumblebee' shit! Hell, man," he said, his voice almost a shout, "Wynton should be gettin' a lifetime salary for playin' that music! I mean, bein' a black person, I don't accept that shit that so-called jazz has stagnated. Old jazz, yeah, but not the new stuff. White people teachin' jazz in schools now. Tryin' to claim it as theirs. But I don't see why our music can't be given the respect of European classical music. I mean, Beethoven's been dead all these years and they talkin' about him, teachin' him, and still playin' his music. Our music is classical. They just don't want to do it because black people started it.

"My point is," he said, biting down on a cheese Danish, "why should black people devote their time to learnin' their music, their operas, their reason for fallin' in love, their reason for committing suicide, the way they fuck, the way they talk, the clothes they wear, their problems, you know what I mean? Damn, at one o'clock on the fuckin' TV, all you can see is them with their hair all fixed up and shit, talkin' about, 'Well, I don't know if Jim's gonna tell me not to go with Irving 'cause my mother used to go with his mother.' That kinda shit! That's not black! We don't sit up there and listen to Billy Graham and that other motherfucka, Bishop Sheen, who be soundin' just like Reagan. No," he said emphatically, "I won't ever do their shit no more and I don't see no honor in no other black person doin' their shit."

giving miles a lift

It was getting dark outside. The sky was almost as gray as the walls and floor of Miles' apartment. He'd grown silent, gone back to drawing again. He asked me if I had a car. I told him I did. He asked if I could give him a lift downtown. I was surprised but told him that I would. He left to get dressed and then we prepared to leave. He told Michael, his valet, that he'd be back tomorrow. Michael nodded his head as Miles and I moved out of the apartment and into the elevator.

On the street, Fifth Avenue, heads turned in recognition when they saw Miles, but no one spoke; they only nodded their heads. He didn't acknowledge them. He was dressed all in black and was walking with that hip-dedip stride. He was wearing dark shades but I could see that his eyes, moving quickly from side to side, didn't miss anything. Nothing. And I was there, too, trying to walk and look as hip as I knew how. When we arrived at my car, a brownish-bronze 1983 Saab 900, he said to me, laughing, "What kind of piece of shit is this?"

"It's the piece of shit that's gonna give you a lift downtown if you keep your mouth shut," I answered right back before I could even think about it.

He kind of grinned and chuckled to himself as he got in. Then he said, "Man, besides being funny lookin', you're about a crazy motherfucka, too. Does the tape deck work?"

"Yeah," I said.

"Well then, turn the motherfucka on," he said again, chuckling to himself. "I wanna play you some real new shit I just recorded. See where your head is at."

I turned the radio and tape deck on and he slid the tape in and pushed the play button. The music bloomed out in waves, music that would later be on his *Tutu* album, the first record he would make for Warner. I liked it and told him so. He just smiled and then looked at me and said, "You know, you're alright, but you still one of the funniest looking motherfuckas I've ever seen."

Then he sank into silence, shaking his head, chuckling to himself, eyes darting here and there behind his dark glasses as we rode downtown through the New York streets. We rode all the way downtown in silence, but when he got to his destination, a large apartment building next to the Hudson River, in an area now called Noho, I got the feeling that something good had happened between us in some weird, edgy, wonderful sort of way. After he got out of my car, he started to walk away, then turned around and walked back up to my car. He looked in, pulled a piece of paper out of his pocket, and wrote something on it. I looked at the paper. It was a telephone number. He told me it was his private telephone number and not to give it to anyone. I took it and said, laughing, "Oh? What do you expect me to do? Walk down the street waving your telephone number in the air saying, Hey, this is Miles Davis' telephone number. Any of you motherfuckas out there want it?"

He looked long and hard at me for a moment, his eyes inscrutable behind his wraparound dark shades. Then he pushed them up on his forehead, and I saw that he was eyeing me humorously, incredulously, as if he didn't believe what he'd just heard. A twinkle flashed into his eyes, and he laughed that sneaky laugh of his under his breath and said, "Man, you sure are a crazy motherfucka. Call me if you need anything else, OK? Later."

He turned and walked away, bouncing up and down in that hip

bop strut of his. When he disappeared into the building, I felt I was on top of the world. I drove off exhilarated, not the least bit tired, feeling like we'd connected in some real meaningful way, though I had no idea what this relationship would lead to. The first thing was to get those tapes transcribed and write a good story for *Spin*. After that, I remember telling myself, whatever happens will take care of itself. And it did.

Yes, it sho-nuff did.

two

up close and personal

The *Spin* article turned out great. In fact, the piece, published in November and December 1985, was the first two-part feature *Spin* ever ran. Rudy Langlais, my editor from the *Village Voice* who had moved to *Spin*, did a fantastic editing job on it. My future wife, Margaret's, criticism was very helpful, too. (She called the first draft "a piece of shit" and it was. So I rewrote it, and she loved the rewrite.) Everyone who read it was knocked out by it. But, most important, Miles loved it. He called me and told me so. After our brief but to-the-point conversation, I was thrilled. I was up there, floating on some clouds. Nonetheless, when the call came through from Bob Bender and Maliaka Adera, both editors at Simon and Schuster, that Miles wanted me to write his life story, I was shocked. Marie Brown negotiated a coauthorship deal for me, and I signed the contract in the spring of 1986 and began spending hours upon hours interviewing and taping him, in New York and at his seaside home in Malibu, California.

getting acquainted

During the summer of 1986, I came to know Miles as almost child-like (which was a shock), delicate (which was a bigger shock), and much softer than I could ever have imagined him being. Of course, he could turn tough and hard again in a flash. One thing was certain: it would have been damn near impossible to take advantage of him because he was always alert to such a possibility from any- and everyone. At first he seemed to be on guard most of the time, even when he was pretty relaxed. Still, if he liked and trusted you, he was quite generous with his time, ideas, and feelings. After we had been working together for a while, he started giving me live tapes of his concerts on the condition that I not give them to anyone else, and I never did.

The most striking thing for me about Miles' physical makeup besides the extraordinarily beautiful color of his deep black skin was his eyes. They were riveting. You could see his resolute sense of self in his eyes, which were large and round, with a lot of white surrounding the iris. When he looked at you, it was with a direct, unflinching, hard gaze. You saw and felt his genius in those eyes. Feminine, like his face, his eyes when he was happy could be very soft, almost delicate. When he was angry, they could be as fierce as his words.

Sometimes, when I was looking at him, he had an almost spiritual, mystical effect on me. I remember looking at his face many times while we were talking and actually hearing some of his tunes, especially "All Blues." I would always hear the music distinctly, clearly, as if it were emanating from somewhere inside his being. It was weird but fascinating. At first, I thought he might be playing a record player in another room. But then I knew that couldn't be true, because Sandra DaCosta had told me that he *never* listened to any of his old music, that, in fact, he loathed even *talking* about the past.

This fact was brought home to me in many of my early interviews with him because it was like pulling teeth to get him to talk about the past, especially about his old music, friends who had died, or his children, whom he always seemed to be protecting. "What chu wanna know *that* for?" he would ask if my question had really bothered him. I would respond that it was his life, but he had "picked me" to write it—so I had to know. Then, over time, he would relent and answer my question, but always grudgingly. After a while, maybe six months or so, he became more relaxed and our conversations flowed more easily. Eventually, he seemed to relish telling me some of the old stories about Charlie Parker, "Philly Joe" Jones, Dizzy Gillespie, Thelonious Monk, and John Coltrane. But he still never played any of the old music.

As I got to know him better, my awe of him was replaced by a healthy sense of respect. In spite of, or perhaps because of, the complexities of his genius and his character, Miles was very unpredictable. He was subject to rapid mood swings, especially after he had injected insulin for his diabetes or had had a bad day. He used to say that the reason his moods shifted so quickly was that he was a Gemini. He enjoyed telling me, "I'm a double six, the Devil, so don't fuck with me." Then he'd smile that mischievous smile of his. I noticed that his most severe mood shifts occurred right after he had taken his insulin shots. If I came around at those times, he would have such a low energy level that he would soon get drowsy and want to sleep. And if I stayed around too long, he'd get edgy, incommunicative, and sometimes downright hostile.

But when his energy was high he could be very funny, with a sly, wicked sort of humor. Like the first time I walked into his Malibu home after I signed the contract to write his autobiography—he cracked me up. He was seated at a table on his beautiful veranda, which overlooked a dazzling flower garden. Beyond the garden, the sparkling blue of the Pacific Ocean shimmered with light that looked like glinting razors or slivers of glass. When I sat down with him, he looked at me and the first thing he said, with a sly grin, was, "I got you a great gig, didn't I? A damn *good* gig." I had to laugh, because he was right. I had heard through the grapevine that he had fought to get me over many other writers because he'd liked my *Spin* piece so much and because he thought I could do the job.

Miles' humor could also have a cold edge when he wanted to make a point. For example, he was always putting down my Saab because he was used to all those expensive foreign sports cars he owned and drove. So about the third time I was scheduled to fly out to California for a work session with him, he told me not to get my usual rental car because he was going to pick me up and show me a *real* car.

When I arrived, there was no Miles to meet me. I wondered where he was. I went down to the carousel to pick up my luggage. No Miles there either. So I picked up my baggage and walked out of the terminal and there, parked by the curb, was Miles in his yellow Ferrari Tesstarosa.

"Get in," he told me, grinning. "Now this is a *real* car, motherfucka. This is the real thing."

"Sure is," I said, smiling, relieved he hadn't forgotten to pick me up.

He sensed this and said, "Thought I wasn't going to be here, didn't you?"

"Yeah," I said, curious as to how he knew. I didn't find out, because the next thing he said was, "You wanna drive this bad motherfucka?"

I was taken aback. I looked at his face, half-hidden by his ever-present sunglasses and asked, "You really don't mind?"

"Go ahead," he said, opening the door and getting out of the car. When I came around the back and passed him, he added, "But you better not wreck it, motherfucka, 'cause you know your poor ass can't pay for gettin' it fixed."

He was smiling again when he said this. He knew he was right. But he was generous in this way—he liked to share what he had with appreciative people.

Outside of the public's relentless scrutiny, Miles Davis was a relatively simple man, a person who loved movies, sports, great food, and all kinds of music. His fame wasn't a big deal to him. If he liked you, he would cook and serve you a great meal and not think anything of it. (He cooked a lot of dishes, but his chili was memorable.)

Miles loved *all* kinds of music. When I went over to his house or apartment, he might be listening to anything—Mozart, Beethoven, James Brown, Prince, Phil Collins—anything except old jazz. He never, ever listened to old jazz because he thought it was dead—even his own older recordings. His new music, yes; he listened to that.

I think Miles felt a detachment from the music of Mozart that allowed him to continue to appreciate it and that was unlike his feelings for old jazz, some of which he had helped to create and which he felt a need to evolve away from into something new. The tradition of African-American music—all of it—has always been to try to move forward, to constantly create new styles and new forms, to live in the present moment and not the past. "Don't look back, someone might be gaining on you," Satchel Paige, the great African-American baseball pitcher, once said, and many black musicians seem to take this statement as an article of faith. That's why most young African-American musicians (and, I might add, music lovers) don't listen to blues, which, like much of jazz, has a white audience—because it's in the past. Rap and hip-hop culture are now the rage because they're in the present, and that's where younger African-Americans' heads are at. Miles was like this, too, always dealing with the present and the future, instead of the past.

Miles liked being alone; he told me that being alone was the price he had to pay to always be open to the flow of his creative juices. To that extent, his isolation was self-imposed. It was something he orchestrated in order to create the space he needed to soliloquize with himself. This isolation kept him focused on his music and painting and helped him elevate his contribution to jazz to high art. He changed his personal style of music and of jazz itself at least six times.

the child in miles

As I said, at times Miles seemed very childlike to me. He once told me he believed that great artists have to retain a childlike fascination with what they do. They have to remain open to the world in the way that children are in order to do the work they do. Miles believed that when artists grow too adult in their thinking and emotions, they lose the ability to let their imaginations run free. Then, they become closed to the many creative possibilities that are always emerging. He thought that young children, especially those of kindergarten age, who are still relatively unburdened by the rules and regulations of the adult world, are free in this regard. He believed that the rules governing adult conduct stifled and eventually strangled creative imagination and expression.

Miles loved my son Porter from the first time he met him. I had described to him how two-and-a-half-year-old Porter used to come into my study when I was writing the piece for *Spin* and go directly up to a photograph of Miles I had lying on the floor and just stare at it. I would tell Porter, "That's Miles Davis," over and over again, and he would just sit there, staring at Miles' face. Porter was fascinated with the photo and over time he began to say "Miles Davis" every time he saw it. I told this story to Miles a few times and he, always on the alert for the con, acted like he didn't believe me. He would say, "Aw, Quincy, you don't have to tell me that kind of bullshit to be friendly with me." I would protest, and swear that what I was saying was true, but he would dismiss the subject with a wave of his hand and we'd go on to something else.

Finally, in the summer of 1987, when Porter was four and a half, Miles called me one Saturday to see whether I was coming down to his apartment on Fifth Avenue. I told him I was planning to and he told me to "bring that boy—I want to see if you been bullshitting me all this time, saying he recognizes me." I said, "OK," and Miles came back with, "And don't tell him you're coming down here to see me, either. I want to see if you've been telling the truth all this time or putting me on."

I laughed, but I wondered whether Porter *would* recognize Miles when he actually met him face to face. If he didn't, it would set me up for Miles to be forever taunting me about being a liar.

Porter and I drove downtown to Miles' place from my apartment in Harlem. On the way, Porter kept asking me where we were going, but I wouldn't tell him. When we got to Miles' place and the valet let us in, Porter ambled into the apartment ahead of me, and there, across the distance of two rooms, standing in full profile in front of the TV set, was Miles. When Porter came in, Miles turned to face him and Porter, adjusting his eyes to the darkness and seeing who it was, started screaming joyfully to me, "Look, Daddy, Miles Davis, Miles Davis!"

A big grin broke across Miles' face and he ordered Porter to "Come here, boy!" And Porter did, running across the room as fast as his little legs could carry him. He jumped into Miles' arms shouting, "Miles Davis, Miles Davis!" Miles loved it and from then on Porter had a special place in his heart.

After that, from time to time I would take Porter with me when I was just going to hang out with Miles. On these occasions, Porter became fascinated with Miles' beautiful red and blue trumpets and would ask him to play them, which Miles did several times. It was a beautiful scene to watch: the legendary trumpeter playing just for the child, with Porter laughing and squealing along with every note Miles played. Miles would be smiling, too, explaining to Porter the different notes he was playing.

As time went on, though, Miles grew tired of Porter asking him to play every time he visited. I could tell this was happening because Miles lost the enthusiasm of his first encounters with my son. One day when Porter and I arrived, the blue and red trumpets were nowhere to be seen. Porter searched all over the apartment for them in vain. Miles and I watched him running frantically from room to room, growing ever more disappointed. Finally, Porter came up to Miles and demanded, "Where *are* the trumpets?" Miles told him they were in Los Angeles. (They weren't; they were hidden high up in a closet because Miles didn't want to play for Porter anymore.)

However, Miles had left his beat-up old trumpet out, and when Porter found it, he asked him to play. At first, Miles refused, saying, "Aw, Porter, I get a lot of money to play this horn. I ain't got time to play it for you today." Upon hearing that, Porter broke down instantly and started to cry. Miles looked at me, startled, and then with a disgusted look in his eyes, he got up, got the trumpet, and played a few notes for the boy. Miles was obviously irritated but he went through the motions anyway. Of course, Porter was delighted. But the next time my son came downtown with me there were *no* trumpets anywhere in sight. When Porter asked about them, Miles said they were all out in Los Angeles and although Porter looked disappointed he seemed to understand. Miles looked at me as if to say, "And don't you tell him they're hidden up in my closet, either." Of course I didn't, and that was the end of Porter's private concerts with Miles; but while they lasted, it was beautiful to watch—and hear.

Although he refused to play for him anymore, Miles continued asking after Porter all the time. Once, in 1988 when I took Porter with me out to the house in Malibu, Miles told him, "Make your dad get you a Ferrari instead of that old beat-up Saab he be driving. Now a Ferrari is a *real* car."

When he told him this, he smiled at Porter as if they were in on some kind of conspiracy together. I told Porter, "Ask Miles to buy you a Ferrari because he's rich and can afford it."

Well, I thought, that was the end of that. But instead of buying Porter a real Ferrari, Miles bought him an expensive red toy Ferrari, an exact replica, which, naturally, Porter completely destroyed in just a few weeks. The boy took it apart piece by piece. First it had no wheels, then the doors went, then the hood. The trunk door was the last to go. When Miles would ask about the toy, I'd tell him how much Porter loved it. I never told him what condition it was in. Not a word. But it was a beautiful toy while it lasted.

at ease among horses

Miles felt at ease not only with children but also with animals, especially horses. I often went with him to the Malibu stables where he kept his horses, just down the road from his home on the Pacific Coast Highway, and watched him ride. He was really at peace with them and treated them with love and tenderness, stroking their muzzles, flanks, and rumps. He would comb their manes, brush their hair, and feed them with such a joyous and serene expression on his face. When he was with them, he was like another person. He trusted animals more than he trusted humans; he told me so on many occasions. And, when I was with him and his horses, I could see that he meant it.

Miles had three horses, if memory serves: Kara, Kind of Blue, and Gemini. Kind of Blue was named after Miles' tune, and Gemini after his sign; I don't know where Kara got her name. I went riding with him once; I rode Kind of Blue and he rode Gemini. He wasn't a great rider but he had a lot of style up in the saddle, trying to look like he was in control. Kind of Blue just tolerated me because I was definitely an amateur, and scared to death. But we rode around at a slow trot for about an hour, with the beautiful mountains of Malibu looming high behind us.

When we rode up one of the trails that climbed the mountain, we could look back and see the sparkling, cold blue water of the Pacific and hear the sound of its power pounding the shore. It was awesome. When I looked at Miles he was smiling peacefully, at ease with himself. I was still scared shitless and this amused Miles to no end; he teased me unmercifully about it later on that evening. Still, the experience remains for me a rare, beautiful moment: Miles and me on horses, the mountains behind, and the sea, in all its power and beauty, making that thundering sound.

miles at work

On our first ride downtown together, in the summer of 1985, Miles had played some tunes for me from the album that would be released in 1986 as *Tutu.* (It was named after the black South African Nobel Peace Prize winner, Bishop Desmond Tutu.) When the album came out, I liked every tune on it very much. I thought it was a first-rate record, one of the best of Miles' last studio albums. *Tutu* was Miles' first album for Warner's, but it didn't feature many musicians from his working band—only Adam Holzman on synthesizer and the bassist Marcus Miller were members of the band. The rest of the musicians were brought in just for the recording date.

A young synthesizer programmer, Jason Miles, whom Miles called "a programming genius," was brought in to coordinate the computer programming of the music, which kept changing constantly. The way it was done was like this: After the arrangers had gotten the percussion instruments, synthesizers, and electric violin parts down on tape, Miles would come into the studio and play his trumpet over the tape-recorded parts. For Miles, who had always played right alongside the other musicians in his bands, this was a totally new way of working. Recording with his working band had become problematic. Miles said the reason he hadn't used that band on *Tutu* was that it was just "too much trouble." He told me: "The band might not feel good the day of the recording session, or, at least, some people in the band might not feel good. So you've got to deal with that. And if one or two musicians don't feel good that day, then they throw everybody else off. Or they might not feel like playing the style you want or need for the record you're doing, and that might cause problems. Music, to me, is all about styles; and if somebody can't do what you ask for and need, then they look at you all funny and feel bad and insecure.

"You've got to teach them what you want them to do, show them right there in the studio in front of everybody else. And a lot of musicians can't take that kind of shit, so they get mad. That holds things up. Doing it the old way, recording like we used to, is just too much trouble and takes too much time. Some people say they miss that spontaneity and spark that comes out of recording with a band right there in the studio. Maybe that's true; I don't know. All I know is that the new recording technology makes it easier to do it the way we have been doing it. If a musician is really professional he will give you what you want in terms of performance in the studio by playing off and against the band that's already down on tape. I mean, the motherfucka *can* hear what is being played, can't he? And that's all that is important in ensemble playing; hearing what everyone else is doing—and playing off or against that."

Tutu was well received by the critics as well as the record-buying public, and it brought Miles a measure of the critical respect that had been missing since his return to the scene. (The album cover, a full-faced black-and-white photo of Miles staring out at the viewer, was plastered all over New York. The picture, taken by Irving Penn, is brooding but beautiful.)

Things were definitely looking up, but Miles was still having problems with his working band. The personnel kept shifting. Musicians kept leaving and returning. His bass player, Marcus Miller, left because he found that he could make more money producing than playing full-time with Miles. He was replaced by a gifted young player from Chicago, Darryl Jones. But Jones left in 1986 to tour with the rock star Sting. John Scofield, Mike Stern, and Robben Ford each played guitar for a while. Darryl Jones came back. Then Marcus Miller sent Miles a tape of a young bass guitarist from Cincinnati, Joseph Foley McCreary. I was at Miles' Malibu house when the tape arrived.

"Listen to this and tell me what you think of it," he said in that whispery voice of his one Saturday afternoon right after I arrived to work on the book. He put the tape in the machine and turned up the volume. We were sitting on his terrace looking out at the sunlit, beautiful Pacific when all of a sudden this Jimi Hendrix–like blast came roaring out of the speakers. I was stunned, but I dug it. The playing was very raw but had a compelling beauty and energy.

"Well," he said, looking at me with his hard, penetrating gaze, "what the fuck do you think?"

"I like it," I said. "It's powerful. He can play."

"Good," he said. "That's gonna be my next guitar player. His name is Foley, and he's gonna be a bad motherfucka."

I agreed. Foley could play his ass off. The only problem I could see was that Darryl Jones was still in the band. But it all worked itself out later when Darryl decided to leave the band for good, which Miles was already anticipating. Miles was a smart man—most times he was ahead of the game.

touchy subjects

On that day Miles was happy, upbeat, telling jokes. But other times he was a very difficult person to get along with. Some days, when things didn't go his way, he was irascible, contemptuous, brutally honest, and extremely bad-tempered. For all his fame and money he was also insecure about many things. He was both proud of being black and totally freaked out sometimes by the deep blackness of his skin and by the hair weave he wore.

Miles told me that his hair began falling out in the late 1960s and early 1970s "because of a hair disease." First, when it was in style, he sometimes wore an Afro wig. Then, as the times and hair styles changed, he began pulling his hair back and covering the bald spots by wearing caps and hats. In the 1980s, he got a hair weave. He was very sensitive about his hair and sometimes if I wanted to scare him I would hold my hands over the top of his head, acting as if I was going to pull his weave out. He would wave his hand over his head frantically as if he were battling a swarm of gnats, smiling nervously and telling me to "knock it off." He never got really mad because he saw the humor in our playful interchange. Still, I think it annoyed him sometimes because his eyes would sometimes flash hard and he wouldn't talk to me for a while.

His skin color was a deeper problem. It's not that he absolutely hated his color. No, that wasn't it. But he did talk about how his deep black color always elicited comments, some good and some bad. He used to tell me how sick he was of people talking about it. "Why can't they just accept it, my color, for what it is?" he once asked me. I didn't have an answer. He also told me he didn't want a woman darker than he was. In our book, *Miles,* he said: "If you ask me what color woman I prefer, I'd have to say I like a woman my mother's color, or lighter. I don't know why that is, but that's the way I am. I think I've had one girlfriend who was darker than me and you know that was dark because I'm midnight black myself."

Many African Americans of Miles' generation, if they were as dark as he, felt deeply inferior because of the hostile manner in which they were treated. An African-American saying from the times went something like this: "If you're black, get back; if you're brown, stick around; if you're white or light, you're alright." Many African Americans from Miles' generation internalized these racist attitudes and turned them into self-hatred. I'm not saying that Miles hated himself, far from it; he seemed to *love* himself as far as I could see, but he might have been deeply troubled by his dark color, over which he had no control, unlike the music he played and composed.

a bundle of contradictions

As I said, Miles was a very complex person. In some social situations he was absolutely unsure of himself. But he was always totally confident of his musical ability, though not, as some have suggested, arrogant about it. In 1986, he was still in awe of Dizzy Gillespie, Charlie Parker, and Duke Ellington, even if he stayed away from listening to their music. He loved James Brown, Prince, and Michael Jackson, and great classical composers, too. He loved barbecue, pig snouts, chili, French pastries, ice cream—in fact, he loved most sweets—and he snuck out to eat these things despite his advanced diabetic condition.

Miles was a bundle of walking, breathing contradictions. He was generous and cheap, stylishly elegant and a "country bumpkin," naïve about many things and completely shrewd and learned about others. For example, although he drew and painted many hours every week, he knew almost nothing about African-American or African art. He knew few artists' names, but he could discuss what he liked and disliked about Pablo Picasso's and Salvador Dalí's work, at length. He was one of the kindest people I ever met and one of the most infuriating assholes, too.

At times, he was extremely funny; at others, unbelievably mean. He could be so humble one moment, and the next moment (and I do mean the very next moment) he could turn into the most exasperating, most obnoxious bastard you could ever hope to avoid meeting. He always used to say, "Everything's about timing." And so it was when it came to Miles—who you got depended on when you caught him and what state of mind he was in. Really.

Miles Davis was a very good actor. When he was with me he was always acting all the time, giving me this and that character—the gangster, the lover, the artist. He had in him a little of Humphrey Bogart, Fred Astaire, Clark Gable, and the legendary black Harlem gangster Bumpy Johnson. Actually, it wasn't acting, really. He had some of all these men *in his character*—he had absorbed them into his very being. He also was always testing me, probing here and there, trying to find weaknesses in my character, in what I believed, trying to see how strong or weak I was. He did this to everyone, and if he found you weak or stupid he would come down hard on you right away and without any mercy. He didn't suffer what he thought was foolishness lightly, or easily. He could be real "cold" on you if he thought you came off wrong.

When you were with Miles and, in his opinion, you came off wrong, you would suffer one of four things. One, he just might completely ignore you. Two, he might take off his glasses and turn his ray-gun, laser-beam eyes on you as if he were trying to execute you with his stare. Three, he just might curse you out, put you down so hard and in such an unbelievably cruel way that you would never, ever repeat what you had just said or done—at least not in his presence. Four, and only if he liked you, he might play with you the way a cat plays with a cornered mouse. In the first three months that I worked on his book with him, I underwent three fierce put-downs for doing and saying things he didn't like: for showing up at his Manhattan apartment for an appointment when he was making love; for calling him on the phone when he was doing the same thing; and for asking him what he considered a stupid question. Three baptisms by Miles' verbal fire.

miles on his mark

While Miles was endlessly contradictory in his life, most of the time he was completely consistent in the quality of the music he played. When it came to music, he was almost always on the mark, on his mark. He knew what he liked and disliked as soon as he heard it and he seldom wavered once he had made up his mind.

I remember bringing by the music of Kassav for him to listen to one afternoon when he was feeling down. Kassav is a West Indian band whose members are mainly from Guadeloupe and Martinique. They lived in Paris then and were playing a form of Caribbean music called "zouk." As soon as he heard them, Miles almost jumped out of his skin with excitement, leaping up from the couch he was lying on and yelling, "Who is that and what are they playing?" He snatched the CD cover out of my hand and tried to read the liner notes, but he couldn't because they were in French. Kassav's music completely freaked him out, and after borrowing the CD from me and listening to it for three days, he directed Larry Blackmon and Marcus Miller to write something for the album they were working on based on Kassav's rhythms and feeling. That album eventually turned into *Amandla*.

Miles was always asking me to bring by music I liked because he said he "trusted" my musical judgment "sometimes." One day he said he was looking for a saxophonist, so I brought over some records by the World Saxophone Quartet. I thought everyone in this group was great. After he heard the music, he rejected all of it right away, saying, "They can really play but they ain't doin' nothin' new in their individual voices that ain't been done before. I like all of them but I can't use none of their individual styles in my band, you know what I mean?"

Yes, I did, and although I disagreed with him, I understood perfectly well why they didn't serve his needs. He wanted—needed—someone younger, someone who hadn't been a leader, who would play his music without question and whose voice spoke to and blended with his. One day a few months later, I went by his place and he told me his new saxophonist was Kenny Garrett. This fabulously gifted young player stayed with his band until Miles' death. Today he is one of the rising stars on alto saxophone in the world of jazz.

I remember another incident with Miles that involved my musical taste. It happened when I went to his Malibu home in August of 1986. It was another one of those fabulously beautiful days

Miles and I always seemed to be spending together. Blue sky. Cool ocean breezes tonguing in. The mountains on the other side of Highway 101 across from his house loomed high and reminded me of Haiti. We were sitting out on the terrace and the sun was extinguishing its fiery self in an orange grave of liquid flames way out to the west. It was a wondrous sight and Miles and I were sitting there silent, just watching. He was chewing gum furiously, as he often did. (Once when I asked him why he chewed so much gum, he said, "Gotta keep my breath sweet for kissin' fine ladies. Gotta be ready if and when the opportunity presents itself.") The Pacific's waves were crashing on the beach just below the terrace. As usual, Miles was wearing black denims, a black silk T-shirt, a black jeans jacket, and wraparound sunglasses. I remember thinking when I looked at him from the side that I could see a lot of Native American Indian in his profile.

This was about three months after I had begun working on the book with him. We were closer. I could feel the friendship growing every time I was with him. But I was still wary of his unpredictable wrath and I didn't want to go through another verbal dressing down. So on that August evening, when we were both silently staring out at the breathtaking sunset, I was carefully choosing the words that I would say to him, running them back and forth through my mind and reviewing them the way a film editor looks at frames.

I remember the darkness swelling up as suddenly as yeast in baking bread. Miles was gulping down great quantities of his beloved Evian water straight from the bottle. He had turned on the terrace lights and was drawing on his drawing pad as on the day of our first interview. All of a sudden he stopped drawing, took off his glasses, and turned those eyes of his on me. They were glittering devilishly. He bit down on the earpiece of his sunglasses, and the corners of his lips twitched playfully as, out of the blue, he asked, "Quincy, what do you think of McCoy Tyner as a piano player? You said you liked Trane. So what do you think of McCoy, brother?"

I sensed a set-up, so I proceeded cautiously. "I like the group sound Trane had when McCoy was in the group," I began.

"Answer the question, motherfucka," he broke in with his rasping, low voice without missing a beat. His eyes were alternately flashing mischief and menace. "Answer the motherfuckin' question! Do you like him or don't chu?"

"I like him, Miles," I said, a little taken aback by his sudden attack erupting after such a long stretch of silence.

"Why?" he asked, after a long, pregnant pause. "Why do you like McCoy as a pianist, Quincy?" He said this sarcastically, with a touch of playfulness giggling around the corners of his words.

"Because I think he plays well," I said, on the lookout now for a verbal sucker punch.

"Oh, 'he plays the piano well,' you say," Miles said, really warming up to the game he had set in motion, really enjoying having me cornered like a mouse.

"Well, are you sure he plays well?" he continued, trying to keep a smile from cracking his face. "And how the fuck would you know he's playin' well? You a trained pianist or something?"

"Naw, I ain't no trained pianist. I'm talkin' about what I like to hear in a piano player," I said, by then more than a little hurt and offended by Miles' attitude and the dilemma I found myself in.

I was especially hurt by all of this because Miles had recently told me, "All musicians aren't great, creative people. Some of them are just technicians and can't hear shit. Now take somebody like you, Quincy; you got *great ears* and can hear your ass off. If you played an instrument you'd be a 'bad' motherfucka, a *really great* musician." I had taken that as a measure of his respect for my knowledge and feeling for music. Now, here he was treating me like a bum, like someone who didn't know the first thing about music, and I was really hurt by it.

"Oh, is that what it is? " he said, almost laughing at me then. "You like what you're hearin'? Well, do you know *what* you're listenin' to? Do you know if his playin' is in context to what everyone else is playin'?"

"Well, Trane must have liked it," I shot back, going on the offensive. "If he was good enough for Trane, then he's good enough for me."

"Aw, Quincy, don't tell me no simpleminded bullshit like that," he said, his eyes completely on fire now. "I'm not askin' you what Trane liked—I know what he liked and why! I'm askin' you what *you* like and if you can't tell me that from deep down inside some kind of conviction, then don't say a motherfuckin' thing, you know what I mean, motherfucka?"

I started to tell him, "I just told you what I liked about McCoy, Miles," but I didn't say it because I realized that I hadn't told him *why* I liked McCoy. I stopped and thought for a moment while Miles' eyes burned into mine, waiting for an answer. I had to ask myself, Did I really like McCoy as a pianist by himself, or did I just like him within the context of Trane's group?

One thing I did know was that I hadn't bought but a couple of records by McCoy since he left Trane's group. So what did that mean? I didn't really know.

"Well," Miles said, quietly, "do you like him, or what? What is it, *brother*?"

He was really being sarcastic by then, a little smile playing openly around his lips. He was enjoying being the cat and me being the mouse.

"I really don't know, Miles," I said after a while. "Plus, I really don't really give a fuck!"

"Oh yeah," he said in a raspy, playful voice that told me he knew I was as mad as hell. "Is it that you don't know, or is it that you know but are afraid to tell the truth because you think I might get mad at you?"

He was laughing out loud, certain he'd got my ass exposed, hanging over a barrel. Whatever the name of the game he was playing, he was right and both of us knew it. I was *truly mad* then, almost to the point of wanting to exchange blows. But I knew he wasn't going to lighten up, so I just played the game out, unwilling to come to blows over an emotional conversation like this, because in the end I had too much to lose.

"Naw, Miles, that ain't it." I sank back in my chair, exasperated to the core, which he knew. "Anyway, fuck you, man," I said, badly needing to try and rescue some of my self-respect. "You just playin' head games with me."

"Oh, yeah," he said, "you think I'm just playin' a game with you? Well, you still haven't answered the motherfuckin' question. So what it be, brother, what is the answer, motherfucka? Answer the motherfuckin' question, brother."

He spat out the word "brother" and turned back to the figure he was drawing.

"Well, Miles, I think he can play," I said halfheartedly, not even believing my own words now that he'd beaten me down so bad.

"Naw, Quincy," he said without looking up. "McCoy can't play shit. All he do is bang around the piano. Just bang around. Never played shit and never will. He's a very nice person, but he can't play no piano to *my* way of listening. I told Trane that, too. But Trane liked him, liked what he was doin', and kept him on. But for me McCoy couldn't play if his life depended on it. Then, again, a lot of people didn't like Trane's playin' in my band. But I did, and that's all that counts."

Then he smiled his sideways smile that meant he was about to let me off the hook, and said, looking directly at me now, his eyes gone soft but still sparkling with mischief, "Quincy, I'm surprised at someone who can hear music as well as you liking someone as bad as McCoy Tyner. Now I'm gonna have to reevaluate what I said about your ears, that you could hear so good and all. Yeah, brother," he said, bringing the discussion to a close and giving me a sly look, "I'm gonna have to think about what I said about your ears. You know what I mean, brother? Yeah, I'm gonna have to *rethink* all of that."

This conversation taught me a lot about Miles Davis and about myself as well. What it taught me about Miles was that he loved to confront people to see if they really believed what they said they believed. Arguing with Miles was like fighting with a great swordsman: he was always thrusting for weakness, both in your character and in your argument. He always kept the pressure on, in his arguments and in his playing as well. If you couldn't stand up to him, he had no respect for you. Sometimes he might play the devil's advocate just to see where you stood, just to see if you would stand up for what you believed. If he found you weak, he would just plunge his sword straight through your heart and keep on steppin' without looking back, because he was a man who didn't seem, outwardly at least, to suffer from guilt.

He taught by example, by the way he conducted himself, by the way he did things, and by the way he created and played his music. He taught his band in the same way he taught me. If you were strong you could stay around; if you weren't you had to go.

What I learned about myself on that August evening back in 1986 was that I had to speak out what I believed and be willing to fight for it. After all, Miles was right: If I liked McCoy so much, why hadn't I played the music he'd made since leaving Trane? Until I met Miles, I had stood up for what I believed in with everyone else, even with my heroes. I had always held my ground. After this scene, I vowed that from then on I would stand up to him, too. And I did, from that point on until his death; and our friendship constantly deepened and his respect for me continued to grow.

homage from the stars

In 1986 Miles and his working band played the Amnesty International concert right outside of New York at the Meadowlands Stadium in New Jersey. It had rained all day and the grounds were wet, but the stadium was jammed to the rafters to hear the likes of such rock 'n' roll stars as U2, Sting, and Peter Gabriel and a whole host of others. I was there, and I remember how famous rock and pop stars like Madonna, Sting, Bono from U2, Peter Gabriel, and Ruben Blades all seemed too afraid to say anything to Miles, who sat backstage as if he had drawn a circle around himself and the chair he was seated in, like the one drawn around the General in Gabriel Garcia Marquez's masterpiece, *One Hundred Years of Solitude.* It was as if that imaginary circle had a sign posted that read, "Do not enter unless invited." So these famous stars hovered somewhere outside of this magic circle enclosing Miles and his chair. Waiting. Waiting for Miles to notice or acknowledge them. And when he would notice them with a tiny, almost imperceptible nod of his head, they would enter the circle, one by one, and squat or get down on one knee to speak with the master, until with another tiny, almost imperceptible nod of his head, Miles would let them know that the audience was over, and it was time for them to leave, which they did immediately. It was something else to watch the respect with which these celebrities approached Miles and to see the great honor and esteem they held him in. They were starstruck by him and were grateful to be in his presence.

Despite all the rain, and the media madness of cameras and bright lights, Miles and his band played very well that day at Meadowlands. The concert was broadcast live all over the world. Carlos Santana, the rock guitarist from Mexico and longtime friend of Miles, played with Miles that day, and they just tore the house down. They left the crowd screaming for more. It was fabulous just to be there, to hear Miles play so well and to watch him being treated as musical royalty by so many of the biggest names in music.

Which reminds me about the time Miles told Andy Warhol to pick up his cape at a fashion show they were both modeling for the Japanese fashion designer Kohshin Satoh at the Tunnel discotheque in downtown Manhattan in 1987. Miles and Warhol had been modeling clothes all evening and it was time for the finale. I had gone backstage into the dressing room after the last models walked down the aisle. I knew the finale was coming up and I wanted to see Miles' last outfit up close. When I'd arrived, Miles had just tried on a magnificent gold lamé outfit with a flowing cape. He was supposed to walk out alone on the stage for this number. He was smiling and enjoying himself and so was Warhol. I remember Andy saying, "Miles, you look so divine!" Miles thanked him graciously and then it was time to make his entrance. As he started walking out of the dressing room, however, he realized his cape was dragging on the floor. So he turned around and fixed Warhol with one of his fierce, withering looks and said, "Andy, pick up my motherfuckin' cape!"

It was a command. There's no other way to put it. But Andy just smiled and said softly, "OK, Miles," and he walked over and picked up the cape's hem, and they both walked out onto the runway. The audience exploded with screams and cheers. I remember noticing that Andy's handlers were appalled to hear their boss addressed that way. But Andy loved it. He had a big smile on his face as he walked behind Miles keeping his cape off the floor. He loved Miles and his music and I could see that he loved being with him like that. For Andy, as with so many others, Miles Davis was royalty. A few weeks later Andy was dead as a result of a botched gall bladder operation.

two "fine" women

By 1986, the much-ballyhooed marriage between Cicely Tyson and Miles Davis was just about over. I knew this from seeing and hearing about all their problems from Miles. It wasn't about any other woman. Miles told me he had never loved Cicely in the physical sense but had felt that she was more like a great friend, or a sister. She was the one who had wanted to get married, and he married because she had, in fact, saved his life. That's what he told me.

He also said they weren't getting along because they had different values. He thought that she wanted to be too controlling.

She wanted to screen the friends and people he saw—including me—and he rebelled. Basically, that's what their separation came down to. Plus the fact that, although Miles was from an upper-class family, he had never had the middle-class values or aspirations Cicely Tyson had. At least that's my read on their differences, based on my conversations with Miles on the subject. In any event, by early 1987, they were living separate lives.

But make no mistake about it, Cicely Tyson did Miles a world of good. He had already had his first stroke in 1981 and his health was critical. When he got together with Cicely, he was a long-time serious diabetic who needed to shoot insulin regularly. His health was at the point where it was "Stop using everything or die." After he met her, he completely stopped drinking and using all drugs. Cicely introduced him to health foods and fresh juices. She helped him to kick all of his habits, including cigarette smoking, by turning him on to a Chinese acupuncturist, Dr. Chin, who treated Miles until his death.

(When we were working on the book, Miles talked me into going to Dr. Chin with him for treatments. I wasn't sick or anything like that; Miles just enjoyed my company, and when I told him that I had never had acupuncture, he convinced me to go. I thought it was weird, all those little needles vibrating in my body. I can't say I felt any different after Dr. Chin's treatment, but today I do go to an acupuncturist for my back and I know that the treatment helps me now.)

Cicely also helped him rebound after the deaths of Charlie Mingus and Bill Evans in 1980. Their deaths had really saddened

Miles, and he was ready to quit everything: he just needed someone to support him and Cicely gave him that support. She helped him get off everything that was killing him and got him to live a healthier lifestyle. She saved his life, and he stayed clean until he died.

After breaking up with Cicely, Miles started seeing a Jewish woman, Jo Gelbard, who was a sculptor, painter, and jeweler. I got to know Jo pretty well and I thought she was a dynamite lady—strong, pretty, spiritual, and sweet, an artist in every aspect of her life. When they met, Miles had already begun doodling and drawing—to keep his hands occupied, he liked to say, so they wouldn't have to pick up a drink or hold a cigarette. It was Jo who encouraged him to stop doodling and start painting seriously every day. It was also Jo who helped deepen his budding interest in art by taking him to museums, galleries, and art openings.

By the end of his life, Miles was taking his painting as seriously as he took his music. During the years I knew him, when he wasn't touring and playing and was staying in his New York apartment, he had this daily routine: He would swim in the morning and then come back and paint for hours into the early afternoon, each and every day. After he was done painting, he would practice his horn and later compose fragments of music that he later built into entire compositions. I watched him go through this routine day after day. Miles Davis was a creature of habit in his everyday life, very focused, very disciplined, and I think that this accounted for his phenomenal success in large measure, along with his great creativity.

spirit talk and premonitions

When Gil Evans died in 1987, his death was a great loss for Miles. Gil Evans was Miles' best friend, bar none. Miles loved him and respected his judgment on many things in addition to music, and Gil loved and respected Miles in return, naming his son after him. When I first started going to Miles' house, he displayed only two photos. He carried them with him each time he moved from New York to Malibu and back again. They were pictures of John Coltrane and Gil Evans. Besides some paintings, mostly by Europeans and Haitians (none of his own), a sculpture piece by Melvin Edwards, and, eventually, a painting of his mother and father, those two pictures were the only images he kept around. That was it.

After Gil died, sometimes when I visited Miles, he would tell me of a conversation he had just had with Gil earlier that day. He couldn't believe Gil was dead. He wouldn't accept it, believed only Gil's flesh had left. At first, I was shocked because Gil *had* died, in the physical sense. But for Miles he had *not* died, not in the spiritual sense. I began to realize then that Miles believed in spirits, in a spiritual presence after the flesh was gone. So, as far as he was concerned, Gil was speaking to him. Every day. Miles also told me of visits from Coltrane, Monk, Philly Joe, Charlie Parker, and especially his mother and father. He would sit there, serenely talking about what they had told him and what he had said to them, without batting an eye. For him, they really had been there, carrying on conversations. He was always smiling when he told me of these exchanges across the divide, his face completely relaxed, at ease. After a while, I used to wonder if he talked to anybody else about these otherworldly conversations, and to this day, I still don't know whether he did. But Miles was like that. He was in touch with things most of us weren't. He saw and understood things differently, and he seemed to feel and know things spiritually, almost to the point of having extrasensory perception.

I remember one evening eating dinner with him in his apartment on 59th Street when the doorbell suddenly rang, and his valet opened the door to a strange black man who appeared to be in his late thirties. When Miles saw the man, he asked him who he was and what he wanted. The stranger said he had come to talk to Miles about working with Gordon Meltzer, Miles' road manager, as an assistant road manager. Miles, looking upset, told the man he was supposed to wait down in the lobby and come up only when accompanied by Gordon. The man said he had known that, but since he had arrived before Gordon, he had just come on up because he had the apartment number. Well, Miles ordered him to go right back downstairs and wait for Gordon.

When Gordon arrived with the stranger in tow, we had finished dinner and were sitting in the very large front room facing the park. Miles, peeved with the man for his having come upstairs alone, immediately told Gordon that the stranger wasn't going to work out. Gordon, who could really handle Miles, responded by saying that what happened on the road was *his* job, that *he* was the expert, that he knew this man was good, and that he needed him. Well, Miles looked at Gordon for a moment, then told him to tell the man to go into the kitchen and get everyone some ice cream. Gordon relayed Miles' request, and the man started walking across the wide front room to the kitchen. Miles pulled up his sunglasses and peered intently at the man as he walked. When he disappeared into the kitchen, Miles dropped his sunglasses back into place, turned to Gordon, and said, "Gordon, he's not going to work out."

"Aw, Miles," Gordon said, a little exasperated. "Come on. Why isn't he going to work out?"

"'Cause he walks out of tempo, Gordon," Miles said with a chuckle. "Can't you see, he walks out of tempo. If we hire him he's gonna drop and break everything."

"Come on, Miles," Gordon said, laughing. "You can't be serious."

"I am," Miles said. "Watch what I tell you. He's gonna break everything."

Anyway, the man was hired and went to Europe with the band. Two weeks later my phone rang and it was Miles, laughing hysterically.

"Quincy," he said, "remember that motherfucka that I said walked out of tempo?"

"Yeah," I said, not knowing what was coming.

"Well, he dropped and broke everything. We had to fire him and get somebody else. I told Gordon but he wouldn't listen to me. I guess he will next time, huh? Later."

And he hung up. I could hear him chuckling just before the line went dead.

back at work

By the end of 1988, the personnel in his band had changed again. Having already added Kenny Garrett on reeds, he brought in Joseph Foley McCreary on lead bass and the great drummer from Washington, D.C., Ricky Wellman. He also fired his nephew, Vince Wilburn, who had been playing drums. Later, Miles said that firing his nephew was "one of the most painful things I ever had to do."

I was in Chicago when Miles fired Vince, and I can tell you it caused a lot of strife between Miles and his sister Dorothy, Vince's mother. She refused to go to Miles' concert in Chicago because she felt that he had embarrassed her son, who had been born and raised in Chicago, in front of all his friends by firing him when he did. Dorothy felt that it was a matter of extremely bad timing. She wanted to know why Miles couldn't have done the firing at a later date. But Miles refused to relent, saying that the music came before family goodwill, and so Vince was out of the band even though it was embarrassing for him. For Miles, the music always came first.

Miles released *Siesta* in 1987. It was the score for a film of the same name set in Spain. The film starred Ellen Barkin and Jodie Foster and was released by Warner Bros. The music echoed back to the sound of *Sketches of Spain* and was produced by Marcus Miller, who arranged and wrote all the tunes except for one, "Theme for Augustine; Wind; Seduction; Kiss," which he cowrote with Miles. The album was dedicated to "Gil Evans, The Master." Here, for the first time in the last years of his life, Miles returned to the music he had played in the past. On the title tune, his style echoed the open horn playing he did on *Sketches of Spain*, an album that I come back to from time to time.

Another big event in 1987 was that Miles' first album for Warner, *Tutu*, won the 1987 Grammy Award for jazz. That year Miles toured all over Europe, South America, Japan, China, New Zealand, Australia, and, of course, the United States, managing during this same time to go into the studio to begin recording *Amandla*, a joyous, exuberant album that was Miles' last real studio effort with some of the members in his working band of the time. The recording, which he finished in 1988 but which didn't come out until 1989, is an amalgamation of many styles, from West Indian zouk and American go-go—a black musical style that emerged in the 1970s and 1980s from Washington, D.C.—to hip-hop, pop, and straight-ahead jazz. Even some elements of fusion found their way into the music. The album has a marvelous cut called "Jo-Jo," named for the new love in Miles' life. This album finds Miles in top form on all the tunes, whether he plays muted or open trumpet.

I think it was in late 1988 that Miles started telling me how much he was getting into rap and hip-hop. He said he had started listening to it because some of the younger musicians in his band, like Ricky Wellman, played it on the bus whenever they were touring. Miles said that at first he hadn't paid much attention to it, but he had gotten to know people like Freddie Brathwaite (better known as "Fab Five Freddie"), who was a rapper, DJ, and graffiti artist, and he had begun to like the sound. He recognized it as a new form—a departure—and then he began to *hear* the new sound in his heart and body. (Max Roach once told me he thought hip-hop and rap were the "first departure in American music since bebop.")

I had been listening to rap ever since 1979, when I moved up to Harlem and the kids from my neighborhood played it and rapped it right across the street from my apartment on 116th Street and Seventh Avenue into the wee hours of the morning. (My apartment was around the corner from where Minton's, the legendary jazz club, had been located in the 1940s and 1950s.) The kids rapped and played their music in A. Phillip Randolph Square, a little fenced-in mini-park between Lennox and Seventh avenues and 116th and 117th streets. The park was a mecca for the neighborhood kids, as it had been for the musicians who played at Minton's, and everybody would come there summer evenings, especially on Saturday nights. Other times, I caught young black kids hustling for money by rapping and break dancing on street corners and on the ferry rides to Staten Island, where I taught on Tuesday and Thursday mornings.

But all that was *outside* the house. In 1979, my daughter Tymmie and my oldest son, Quincy Brandon, ages fifteen and thirteen respectively, came to live with Margaret and me and brought the music *into* our house.

So by the time Miles started talking to me about it, I had been listening to it for nine years. He said he wanted to do a record mixing rappers and electronic music with Brazilian and Caribbean beats, especially zouk. He told me once that he was going to talk to Quincy Jones about the project, but whether he ever did, I don't know. Although Miles didn't know a lot about rappers, they knew a lot about him. I used to hear them mentioning his name and talking about how "bad" they thought he was, how creative, how he was "the joint."

That same year, on November 13, Miles was inducted into the Knights of Malta at the Alhambra Palace in Granada, Spain. But by the end of 1988, Miles was in bed, floored by bronchial pneumonia, which the tabloid *The Star* reported as AIDS. He was so sick he had to cancel his winter tour, which he said cost him "a million dollars."

a mysterious virus

He was laid up in a hospital in Santa Monica, with tubes up his nose and in his arms, and needles everywhere. He said about that hospital stay, "Anyone who came into my room had to wear a mask because there was a danger I could be infected by germs brought in by visitors, or even by doctors or nurses. I was pretty sick, but I didn't have AIDS like that bullshit gossip rag *The Star* said I did. Man, that was a terrible thing that paper did to me. It could have ruined my career and fucked up my life. That story made me madder than a motherfucka when I found out about it. It wasn't true, of course, but a lot of people didn't know that, and they believed the story."

When I was writing his autobiography with him and Miles told me this, I didn't know what to believe. I had read the story in *The*

Star, too, and I had heard Miles blame Cicely Tyson for leaking it. He thought she did it to get back at him over the breakup of their marriage. I once asked him point-blank if he had AIDS, and he angrily denied it. I do know that he was always suffering from bad cases of some mysterious flu-like virus that sometimes confined him to bed, without visitors. Also, a short time after the story in *The Star* appeared, when I asked him about some pills he was taking, he said they were AZT. Now, AZT, as is well known, is the drug widely taken for AIDS. I don't know whether he was pulling my leg or not when he told me the name of the pills, but I do know that when I asked him, "Isn't AZT the drug used for AIDS?" he clammed up and told me, "It's none of your business," which it wasn't. So I never brought it up again. Later on, he told me that he had had a complete blood change, somewhere in Switzerland, to clean up a virus he said he was carrying. When I asked what the virus was, he told me again, "It's none of your business." I didn't bring up the subject again after that.

Whatever the truth was, whether Miles had AIDS or not, it wouldn't have made a difference to me. I do know that he had relationships with many women. I met many of them myself. It was also rumored that he had homosexual relationships with friends like his hairdresser, James Fenny—who died of AIDS after Miles passed away—and his former drummer, the late Tony Williams. I never saw Miles in a homosexual relationship, although I *can* say that he had many close homosexual friends, including Jimmy Baldwin, Fenny, the dancer George Faison, the late great Italian fashion designer Gianni Versace, and others. But so do most artists. Me included. He never "hit" on me during the entire span of our relationship.

(I felt I had to address this issue in this book because so many different people have asked me whether Miles died of AIDS. I say that I don't know and that the question should be put to his physician, not to me. What I *can* say is, as far as I'm concerned, it doesn't matter; what mattered for me then and matters to me now is the music he played and my friendship with him.)

the studio museum interview

During the fall or winter of 1988, some friends at the Studio Museum of Harlem asked me whether a public discussion / interview could be arranged between Miles and me for their series "Vital Expressions in American Art." I told them I would ask Miles, and when I did, to my surprise, he agreed to do it. The Studio Museum people were ecstatic. Miles had never done an interview in front of a live audience before, but he said he would do it because he knew of the museum's work with African and African-American visual artists and he wanted to help them in any way he could. When they offered to pay him, he told them to keep the money as a donation. It was a nice gesture and one that Miles did on a regular basis for people and institutions he believed in; he just didn't announce his generous gifts to the public.

In the spring of 1989, the buzz began to go out all over New York's cultural wires and, for those in the know, all around the country's wires, too, that Miles and I were going to sit down and do a live interview at the Studio Museum. All the tickets sold in a flash. For days, Miles kept telling me about how nervous he was because he had never done anything like it before. I kept reassuring him that he should think of it as just playing a concert. But this didn't work at all, because most of the time he hated talking about himself, even in private situations. So the thought of talking about himself in front of a live audience—who would also be asking him questions—was not exactly appealing. Suffice it to say the man was terrified.

When the big night arrived, Miles and I met at his apartment and drove up to Harlem together in his limousine, along with his road manager, Gordon Meltzer. There were so many people outside, we had to go in by the back door to avoid the crush. Some accounts said that about five thousand people were turned away. I was told later that some people were so pissed off about not being able to get in that a riot almost took place.

Once inside the museum, we were ushered—along with my wife, Margaret, who met us there—up to the green room on the second floor, where the trustees and board members were gathered. The museum staff had laid out a spread of cheeses, fruit, bottled water, and juices on a long table. The people there were delighted to see Miles and they greeted him with pleasure. He was gracious and told them all how nervous he was. It was all going very nicely until an elegantly dressed, beautiful black woman and her husband came up to speak to Miles. The woman extended her hand in greeting and said she was so happy Miles had graced them with his presence. He shook her hand and watched her warily from behind his dark glasses. She went on to say that many people had thought that Miles wouldn't show; that although she was a board member, she hardly ever came to anything at the museum; that she was here tonight because she considered this the high point of the museum's history.

Margaret, Miles, and I were shocked when we heard her say this, but Miles responded to her immediately with, "This is a great place, and I wouldn't have you on my motherfuckin' board if you didn't show." And with that he clammed up.

The woman was stunned. Her husband looked as if he wanted to say something but he thought better of it, so they turned around and left the room, as Miles was saying under his breath, "Bourgeois sorry-ass tired black motherfuckas." Everybody in the green room heard the exchange but nobody said anything about it. It was deep.

Then it was time to go downstairs and do the interview. Miles told me again how scared he was. With a nervous grin playing around his mouth he said, "I don't know why I let you talk me into doing this." But he was doing it. My longtime friend Pat Cruz, the wife of the painter Emilio Cruz, had given us both fabulous introductions while we were upstairs. When the crowd saw Miles standing at the top of the stairs, following after me, applause and cheers erupted like you wouldn't believe, because the audience had not been sure that he would show up, either. He was all decked out in a purple silk flowing shirt and black balloon pants that pegged around his ankles, his black wraparound sunglasses securely in place.

Because of Miles' nervousness, the interview started off slowly, but it picked up speed after he felt the crowd was with him and he relaxed. Then he told some great stories about Charlie Parker, James Brown, Prince, Max Roach, and John Coltrane. He talked about how the sound of dribbling a basketball was a rhythm he sometimes used in his music, in his playing. He talked about African-American history and art, about how if black children knew about their African history, then they wouldn't feel so disconnected in America.

He commented on his own drug use, how it had almost destroyed him, what a scourge it was in the African-American community, and the need for our young people to stay drug-free.

He was really funny, wise, and informative for about an hour and a half. The people fortunate enough to be there that night were absolutely enthralled, and they asked questions that he freely answered. He was playful with me and showed a side of his personality that most people never expected to see, or even knew existed. He was fabulous, and that thoroughly integrated audience (it looked like the United Nations) applauded like crazy when he finally said, "Can I go now, Quincy?" We gave each other high fives and hugged and he left, just like that, signing autographs as he made his way back up the stairs.

I was really proud of him that evening, proud that he was able to overcome his fear and pull it off. The next day, after I told him how great he had been, he told me he was "glad he did it" but that he wouldn't do it again. I took him at his word, even when the question came up about whether he would do a book tour to support our book. I told the editors at Simon and Schuster that he wouldn't tour or give talks or sign books. They didn't believe me, and when he refused to do it, bad feelings developed between Miles and the company.

In the end, I had to go out on the road and do the book tour on my own. Many people were disappointed when I showed up without Miles, especially in our hometowns of St. Louis and East St. Louis. But the book sold extremely well, reaching the best-seller lists in several newspapers, most notably the *New York Times*, *San Francisco Chronicle*, and *Village Voice*. But I have no doubt the book would have done even better if Miles had relented and done the tour.

the radio project

In 1989, radio producer Steve Rowland and I came together around an idea that I proposed to him about doing a Miles Davis radio show. After first refusing, Miles finally agreed to participate after I convinced him that it would be a historic event. The end result was a seven-part series, "The Miles Davis Radio Project," narrated by Danny Glover. Steve Rowland and I, along with Jay Allison, won a 1990 Peabody Award for excellence in radio broadcasting for the series. But it was an incredibly taxing and difficult project. In the end, it cost me my friendship with Steve Rowland, whom Miles quickly grew to detest. Now, I'm not saying that the fact that Miles disliked him so intensely was Steve's fault, because Miles could be a very irascible, contemptuous, and difficult person to get along with. But the truth is that Miles *did* dislike Steve, and he disliked him intensely. Let me relate a couple of instances here to illustrate my point.

During the summer of 1989, Steve and I went out to Miles' house in Malibu to tape him. Miles' family was visiting. His sister Dorothy, his brother Vernon, and his nephew Vincent were there—by this time Dorothy and Vincent had patched up their bad feelings with Miles over his firing of Vincent. I knew all of them from having worked on the autobiography—I had finished the book in October of 1988—so when we first got there everything went real well. Dorothy had cooked a meal and we all ate together. Miles and I were kidding around. Everything seemed to be going great, except that from the first moment we walked in, I could tell Miles didn't like Steve Rowland. He just didn't like him. Miles was like that; he could dislike someone at the drop of a hat. He either liked or disliked you instantly, and there was nothing that you could do when he had it in for you. Later, Miles told me that he didn't like Steve's vibe. But he overcame his initial dislike and decided to go ahead with the interview, although by then, I knew Miles well enough to sense that we were in for trouble.

We started out with me interviewing Vincent. Miles' sister and brother declined to be interviewed for the show. Then it was Miles' turn. Now, first of all, you have to remember how much Miles hated to be interviewed, even by me. But he had managed to put his dislike aside and was doing it as a favor to me. Everything started well, with me asking him questions and him answering with verve and humor. Then, about half an hour into it,

I saw Steve's forehead wrinkling with concern as he listened to the sound through his headphones while he was twisting the knobs of his tape recorder. He seemed agitated about something. Knowing that Steve was a perfectionist about any little disturbance in the sound balance, I began to get worried that he would stop the interview because of some technical problem or other, which I *knew* would upset Miles and possibly end the interview. So I frevently hoped Steve wouldn't do that.

All of a sudden, I saw him taking off his headphones and walking over to where we were sitting. Miles was smiling at me when Steve came over and didn't see him approaching. When Steve got there, he told us we had to stop because there was "a little glitch" in the sound that was coming through. Miles looked at him and I saw a dark cloud of fury gathering in his face. Vince, sitting close by, saw it, too. I watched his face kind of flinch with concern. Then Miles said something like, "Well, you're an engineer, aren't you? Why can't you wipe it out *after* we get through talking? What's the big problem here?"

"I just want it to be perfect, Miles," Steve said. "So could we just pick up somewhere in the middle of the last question? You think you could remember what you said before? Because that was a great answer, man!"

Miles looked at me and then at Vince as Steve walked back to his tape recorder and put his headphones back on. Then Steve gave me a signal to begin, which I did by asking the same question again. Miles looked *real* pissed off. He answered the question, though not as well as he had before. But about five minutes into the interview—I could see it coming—Miles ripped off his headphones and called a halt to the proceedings. He said he wanted to talk with me, privately. I looked at Steve with a look that said, "I told you so" on my face, and I followed Miles, who was walking down the hall in the direction of his garage. When I caught up with him he turned, looked me straight in the eyes with that fierce gaze of his, and said, "What's wrong with your boy?"

"Well, Miles," I began, "you know, you make some people nervous. Plus, Steve just wants to make it good, that's all."

"He can clean that shit up in the studio, man. Why he fucking with me and you like that? It's disrespectful. I don't like the motherfucka anyway, never did, never will. He's got to go, and I mean right now. You can stay. We gonna have dinner, watch some movies, listen to some of my new tapes, OK? But that motherfucka's got to go."

He said that with intense finality. But I countered with, "Well, you know, Miles, I drove both of us out here, so Steve doesn't have a way to get back to Los Angeles."

Without blinking an eye or missing a beat, he shot back with, "Well, you go, too, and come back either later or tomorrow. But that motherfucka's got to go. Now!"

Having said his last word on the matter, Miles turned and walked away, leaving me speechless. When I informed Steve that we had to leave, he got really pissed off, too. He tried to tell me that we were paying Miles ten thousand dollars to participate in this program and so he was obligated to sit for the interview.

I told Steve that Miles didn't have to do anything he didn't want to do, that he would give back the money we had given him and that would be the end of the project. When Steve heard that, he calmed down, and we left to begin the long drive back to the Silverlake area of Los Angeles, where we were staying with friends of mine, Teresa and Walter Gordon.

There were other incidents with Steve, like the time Miles threw him out of his rehearsal studio in New York. But when I begged Miles to let us turn the tape recorder on, we still managed to tape the live rehearsal, and it became one of the highlights of the radio series. Steve got very angry over this latest rebuff, and I understood where he was coming from. It's just that Steve's anger wasn't going to change anything, and in the end Steve persevered, got the program finished, and did a great job.

Still, as I said, our friendship didn't survive the heavy-duty stress of putting together this monumental program. I've talked to him only once since we had a transatlantic screaming argument over the phone in the summer of 1990. I was in Prague doing shows for the Travel Channel, and he was in Philadelphia, where he lives. The argument was over my failure to deliver some text for the program. From my point of view, the timing was wrong, and I just couldn't get it in on time. I accept the blame. It is a shame it came down to this breakup after all the hard work we put into the "Miles Davis Radio Project." But that's what happened, and Steve Rowland and I haven't spoken to each other since.

with bassist Paul Chambers

in his dressing room with Annie Ross, circa 1957

with Paul Chambers at the Apollo Theatre, 1960

at the Jazz Workshop in Boston, circa 1966

in New York City, circa 1960

in 1968

with Dizzy Gillespie

at a photo shoot, 1981

with Cicely Tyson, 1983

clowning with photographer Judy Schiller, 1986

in 1990

jamming with Joseph Foley McCreary

recording *Kind of Blue,* with (from left) John Coltrane, Cannonball Adderley, and Bill Evans, 1959

same session, with Paul Chambers on bass

davis versus marsalis

In June of 1989, Miles played Avery Fisher Hall for the Kool Jazz Festival. It was a double bill, with Miles sharing the limelight with Wynton Marsalis. The tickets went in a flash because every jazz buff and his mama in the Big Apple (and elsewhere, too) was salivating over the chance to experience these two trumpet players together on the same bill and to see, hear, and compare the two acknowledged titans of American classical music—jazz.

Wynton had once been one of Miles' many disciples, but in 1989 he found himself at odds with the master over Miles' continued use of the rock and pop musical vocabulary and his use of electrical instruments instead of acoustic ones. They also had different philosophies about the direction jazz should be taking. Miles wanted jazz to continue to evolve, so he married funk, rock, pop, blues, and classical European music with rap, zouk, reggae, and sounds from Brazil, Africa, and East India. Wynton felt jazz should stay classically oriented, in the best tradition of 1960s bebop and hard bop. This disagreement produced a split between the two men.

So this concert was an opportunity for fans to hear both musicians in the same evening and to see who would prevail.

I wasn't there for the first set, which Miles opened, so I don't know what Miles played, but it must have been the set that the *New York Times* music critic Peter Watrous heard and gave an unkind review to, because the second set was simply fabulous. When Margaret and I arrived, people were streaming out of the auditorium at the end of the first set, and there was a definite buzz in the air.

As always, Miles drew the hippest of hip crowds. Everyone was dressed in their very finest—or, as Miles loved to say, everyone was as "clean as a broke-dick dog." His concerts were almost like fashion shows, with everyone watching what everyone else was wearing, which was Issey Miyake, Donna Karan, Gucci, Armani, and Versace, flowing silks, fine linen, "fly" Italian shoes, "slick" bracelets, and hip earrings—you name it, they had it on. Margaret and I were dressed in black Italian jackets—mine, by Benassi E. Vaccari, went well with my hip, blooming, peg-legged pants by Marithe Girbaud.

Miles had gotten me two of the best tickets in the house, three rows from the stage, front and center.

Wynton played a very good opening for the second set, but he talked too much, giving lectures on the blues, on this and that to people who didn't need to hear them; we had come to hear him play, not talk. After Wynton's set and the intermission, everyone filed back in for Miles' second set.

When the stage went dark, signaling the time for the Prince of Darkness to appear, an electrical current of excitement went through the packed house. After he was introduced offstage with the simple line, "Ladies and gentlemen, Miles Davis!" the dark hall was pierced by the sound of his plaintive, mournful, disembodied trumpet, coming from somewhere backstage. He was playing a tune called "New Blues," with no accompaniment. His mute was on, but he was playing wide open, his sound filling up the hall with stark, lonely notes played with deep feeling. The hall was completely quiet. It was mesmerizing to hear him without seeing him, in that absolute silence.

By the time Miles came bopping out with that gimp-legged strut of his and walked into a single spotlight—still playing alone, but having switched from the mute to an open bell, dressed in billowing black silk pants pegged at the cuffs, a black T-shirt covered by a black-and-white checked jacket, and, of course, his wraparound space-cadet shades—he was playing so fine that everyone was stunned into silence. When he finished this a cappella blues solo, the audience gave him a standing ovation. I remember thinking to myself, "Miles sure knows how to make an entrance." And this one was so good it had wiped whatever Wynton had played right out of most people's minds. Then the rest of the band joined him, one by one, walking slowly onto the stage: Joseph Foley, lead bass; Kenny Garrett, alto sax and flute; Ricky Wellman, drums; Kei Akagi, keyboards; Benny Rietveld, bass; and Muyungo Jackson, percussion.

With a single nod from Miles, the band kicked into a tune entitled "Intruder," played at an astonishingly fast tempo. The transition Miles made from slow blues to an ass-kicking up-tempo song was stunning. Miles and Garrett traded fours in the middle of the piece, an antiphonal tour de force that brought the packed house to its feet again. It went on like that for the rest of the set, with one gem after another. The band and Miles played so wonderfully that Wynton's entire band—but without him—came and stood in front of the stage listening, their eyes bugged out, their mouths wide open. It was unforgettable. After one amazing solo, Miles walked to the lip of the stage in front of Margaret and me, pulled up his wraparound shades, and smiled and winked at us. It was beautiful, something Margaret and I will never forget. When the concert was over, people rose to their feet again, applauding, cheering, and whistling like crazy. It was an incredible evening of music.

cloud nine

When our book, *Miles: The Autobiography*, finally came out in late September of 1989, it received a great deal of attention. *Amandla* had just been released to great critical acclaim the month before and was selling very well. The album ignited interest in the book, and a large spread on Miles—with an excerpt from the book—in *Vanity Fair* also helped. Miles and I were on cloud nine.

But not all of the attention was positive. The book was quite controversial because of what Miles had to say and how he said it. Many people objected to what they thought was his excessive use of profanity, and they came down hard on *me* for not editing it out. But that's the way Miles talked. Some readers were angry and disappointed about the way he revealed himself to be an occasionally harsh and brutal person. But he was like that, too. He told the truth in our book, and I deeply respected him for not trying to whitewash his life. That took courage. Still others hated that he shattered their perception of his "cool" persona by coming clean and being truthful about so many unpleasant parts of his life. It was as if he was deconstructing his own myth and legend. This left many of his admirers unhappy because they would have preferred to continue to believe in the mythology about Miles that they had constructed. Most people want their heroes to be perfect. Many readers didn't like the idea that Miles was just another flawed human being. Some readers would have preferred for Miles to have kept his mouth shut about some of the facts he revealed in the book, especially his treatment of women. I know this is so because a great many of his fans told me that.

But the majority of those who read the book loved it for the same reason that it was hated: for Miles' truthfulness and his language. I know one thing for sure: almost every musician I knew read the book—most of them two or three times—and it was a big hit with them.

For many, the book instantly became a classic, reaching almost cult status. Readers told me so everywhere I went. It was amazing. I know it increased the audience for my own work, because sales went up for my books of poetry after it was published. It also didn't hurt my sales one bit that Bill Moyers did a profile of me for his award-winning PBS series on poets, "The Power of the Word," which came out that same September. Suddenly, I seemed to be everywhere. That kind of exposure is something that most contemporary poets never experience in their lifetimes, with the possible exceptions of the late Allen Ginsberg and Amiri Baraka. Much of my name recognition as a poet was due to my co-authorship of Miles' book and the Moyers PBS series.

Miles loved the book. He told me so on many occasions. As a matter of fact, when I delivered the manuscript to him for his final perusal in October of 1988, he called me after he had read it, laughing hysterically and wanting to know how I had managed to nail his speaking voice, his inflections and cadences, as I had. Hearing him say how much he enjoyed the book was a very happy moment for me. Truly. I had worked hard on it, going to Haiti in the spring of 1988 to be alone with Miles' words on tape and in transcripts so I could absorb the rhythms and subtleties of his speech. I broke three typewriters (manual and electric) working on the book.

I had interviewed scores of people to get their takes on Miles. I wanted readers to feel as though they were sitting across from Miles and he was talking directly to them. That's the kind of intimacy I was after. I wanted it to seem like a one-on-one exchange, with him telling his story directly to each and every reader. I believe I achieved that.

I wrote the entire book without showing it to Miles until I had finished with it. I told him this at the beginning, that this is how I work, that I put everything in, warts and all. He agreed to this process, though he did bug me from time to time to let him see it. I refused, because I thought showing him would slow down the process. After a while he stopped asking.

Miles accepted the book as it was because, as he told me, "it was the truth." He did worry some ove the way the book portrayed his treatment of women, but when I reminded him that this portrait was accurate, he didn't protest. The only changes he made were when he disagreed with a date or fact.

I loved doing the book. I loved organizing it. In the end, to get the language straight, I almost had to become Miles, sort of the way an actor becomes a character. In order to get Miles' spirit down on the page I absorbed a lot of his behavior and personality, for instance, his curtness on the telephone and his cryptic comments on almost everything. After I finished the book, I had to separate myself from him, deprogram myself, so to speak. I had to force myself to stop talking like him in order to get back to being myself.

The reaction of some of the critics, however, was perplexing. Some felt that the first part of the book had much richer portraits of people like his father, mother, Charlie Parker, John Coltrane, Philly Joe Jones, and others than the later parts. That was true. But there was a reason for that difference. During the latter part of his career, Miles was not particularly friendly with most of the musicians who played in his bands, with the exceptions of Herbie Hancock, Wayne Shorter, Tony Williams, Ron Carter, Mtume, and Al Foster, with whom he was very close. The portraits of many of the later players were sketchier because Miles didn't hang out with them and, consequently, he had fewer stories to tell. Some critics didn't like the book for other reasons and that was OK; that's their right, and their job.

One of the funny things that happened around the publication of the hardback edition had to do with the picture of Miles smiling on the back cover. He hated seeing himself caught smiling in photos, so we, the editors and I, conspired to keep him from seeing a proof of the back cover picture, which was shot by the French photographer Gilles Larrain. Miles equated smiling in public with black Uncle Tomming. He hated seeing Louis Armstrong, Charlie Parker, and Dizzy Gillespie smiling or laughing in public. So he was determined he wasn't ever going to be photographed while smiling. In public he always kept his tough-guy, no-nonsense mask in place. But I thought the photo would show his fans a more human, likable side of him, which I thought would be good for marketing. It was—but he hated it. He called me up shortly after he got his copy, and cursing and spitting into the phone, he demanded to know what my involvement had been in selecting the picture. I denied having anything to do with it, which he didn't believe, going on to rave about a conspiracy to make him look like an Uncle Tom and a fool. I tried to humor him but he hung up the phone so hard that it made my ears ring for days. Miles could be very gentle, loving and funny, and he smiled a lot. It was just that he didn't want the public to see that side of him. Ever.

It was an honor and a privilege for *me* to have been selected by him to write his book, and I still feel that way today. Miles and I became even closer friends after the book was published. He was always inviting me down to his place to eat and talk. Once the burden of doing interviews for the book was lifted, we could do other things, like watch sports, listen to music, and talk art and politics together. I used to bring him food cooked by a friend of mine, Verta Mae Grosvenor, a commentator for National Public Radio and a great cook. Verta was staying with Margaret and me at our Harlem apartment, where she was cooking all the time, and from time to time I would take some of it to Miles. He loved Verta's cooking so much he used to scheme to try and get some of it every day, especially her great seafood dishes, okra, greens, and cornbread. Of course, I couldn't be going to see him every day, and neither could Verta be cooking for him on a regular basis. But that didn't keep him from trying.

saying good-bye to sammy

Sammy Davis Jr. and Miles were very good friends and had been for a long, long time. In 1990, Sammy Davis was dying of cancer; everybody knew it. There had been several tearful tributes to the great entertainer on television, and everybody who knew him was making a pilgrimage to his Beverly Hills home. But Miles was agonizing whether he should go to see his friend when he was in such bad condition. Miles kept talking about how many of his close friends had died, how much he missed them, and how he wanted to remember Sammy as he was when he was healthy. I stayed out of it, just listened. One day he asked me what I thought. Should he should go to see Sammy or not? He looked me right in the eye, like he always did when he wanted an answer to a question, so I told him I thought he should go see his friend. And he did.

When Miles returned to Manhattan, we talked on the phone, and I went downtown to have lunch with him. Over chili, he began laughing when he started telling me about his visit to Sammy. He described how morose everyone was in Sammy's house, how it felt like a death watch, and how it made him feel so sad. Then, when he went in to see Sammy, he thought on how thin Sammy was, who was always a skinny man, and how big his head looked atop that tiny body. Miles said he could think of nothing else to say, so he just spoke the truth; told him what he was thinking right then and there, saying, "Goddamn, your head look so *big,* Sammy, sitting on top of that tiny little body. Man, you betta eat something, 'cause you look real weird right now."

He told me that everyone in the house was appalled at what he had just said, but that Sammy had instantly broken into hysterical laughter when he heard Miles' words; that Sammy laughed so hard, for so long, tears running down his face, that Miles got worried.

"I felt like he was gonna die on the spot, because his tiny body just shook so hard, his big old head was just rolling around on top of his tiny, tiny body like it was gonna fall right off! Man it was *something else* to see."

Miles added that Sammy called him the next day to thank him for bcing so truthful and for bringing some much needed laughter into his final days. Shortly after, Sammy passed away, and Miles told me he was glad he had been able to lighten his friend's last hours.

margaret the voodoo woman

As mentioned earlier, Miles had been suffering from recurring bouts of a flu-like virus ever since 1985. If my memory serves me right, ever since I'd done the *Spin* story, he had been periodically struck down by the disease and by the side effects of his serious case of diabetes. Now, at the end of 1989, he was under the weather again with the virus, and it put him flat on his back for a longer time than was usual. This time he told me he was suffering from pneumonia. After he recovered from the illness, he went down to play four nights in Pointe-à-Pitre, Guadeloupe. It was the first time he had played on a West Indian island and he loved it, loved his reception there. I felt good about him doing these concerts because I had helped to arrange them through contacts with longtime friends of mine on the island. Those four nights he really killed them down there, and they really *loved* him.

Miles paid for Margaret and me to come down and be with him on the last night of the engagement. The morning after his last concert we looked down from our hotel terrace overlooking the beach and saw him in his bathing suit peering around from behind a bath house, seemingly trying to figure out whether he should go in for a swim, though he didn't.

When I saw him later, I asked him why he hadn't gone in because I knew how much he loved to swim. He just laughed and said, "Oh, you saw me, huh? Well, I was just tryin' to figure out if all them people out there on that beach knew who I was, and if they did, would they come up askin' me for autographs like the Japanese people always do. I didn't want none of that shit, so I just sat there and watched. Man, that was a beautiful beach with some gorgeous ladies on it. Did you and Margaret go in?"

"Yeah," I said.

"How could you stand it?" he said, looking at me quizzically."

"Stand what?" I said, not understanding what he meant.

"Them 'bad,' beautiful women, man. They was finer than a motherfucka. How could you stand it? Not looking at them and shit. I bet it was Margaret, right?"

"Right," I said, smiling.

"Yeah, you got that right. Margaret's a voodoo woman. She would have beat your ass if she caught you looking at all them foxes. Man, I know *I* wouldn't want to get on her bad side."

"You got that right," I said. "And I don't." Then we both cracked up and gave each other high fives.

Miles had given Margaret the nickname "voodoo woman" one afternoon when we were at his New York apartment in the former Essex House Hotel on 59th Street. We were over visiting and eating, and he was about to begin painting. Knowing of our interest in art, he rolled out a couple of paintings and said to Margaret, "Now, see here, what I'm doing here is trying to put some figures up here with a little color."

He went on, pointing to the upper right-hand corner of the painting, "See, the colors kind of merge with the figures. Can you see that, Margaret?"

A little smile of condescension was playing around the corners of his lips like Margaret didn't know what he was talking about. Margaret, a quiet but forceful and, when necessary, outspoken woman with a deep knowledge of art—she has an art gallery today in San Diego—said, "Aw, Miles, you don't have to show me how to look at a painting. I can see. I have a lot of paintings at home. I know a lot about art, probably more than you do."

This shocked Miles. Hardly anyone ever expressed disagreement with Miles. He looked up, his eyes bugging out of his head and said, "Well, excuse me." Then he asked, this time with a little hesitation in his voice, "Well, what *do* you think about it?"

"Well," Margaret said, looking straight at him, "it's alright, but it could use a little work."

"What?" Miles said, a little taken aback, a little angry, but with some humor and surprise in his voice, that smile still playing around his lips. "Well, why don't you let me see some of *your* fucking paintings?"

Everybody laughed then, and Miles looked at me and asked, "How do you live with her?" grinning and looking at her as if he was seeing her in a new light, really seeing her for the first time. Then he said, "She's a voodoo woman. That's what she is: a voodoo woman."

After this incident Miles had nothing but respect for Margaret and treated her accordingly every time he saw her. Most people told Miles what they thought he wanted to hear, but Miles respected only those who honestly spoke their mind.

There was another revealing incident that occurred when Miles invited Margaret and me to the old Essex House apartment to eat his beloved barbecue with him. While the three of us were eating the ribs, Miles brought out a bottle of French red wine that he said had cost six hundred dollars and asked if we wanted some. Remember, by that time, he didn't drink at all. He said he had been given a case by some rich fan. We said, "Sure," so he opened the bottle, and being red wine lovers, Margaret and I began drinking like our lives depended on finishing every last drop. When Miles discovered we had finished the whole bottle, he said, a little perturbed but laughing his way through it, "Goddamn, you motherfuckas must not have ever had no wine like that. Shit, that fuckin' wine cost six hundred dollars and y'all done drunk it up like that?"

"Yeah," Margaret said, "it was real good. You ought to have some."

"You know I can't drink because of my diabetes problem," he said, looking a little sad. "I like to watch other people drink and enjoy it, though."

"That's why we drank it," I said, "so you could watch us. You don't drink, so somebody had to drink it, and it might as well have been us."

"Fuck y'all," he said, half smiling. "You motherfuckas just greedy, that's all." Then he popped a cough drop in his mouth to relieve a coughing fit that came down on him all of a sudden.

"Do those cough drops have sugar in them?" Margaret asked him, mindful of his diabetes.

"No," Miles said. "They're natural and sugarless."

"Let me see the package they came in," she said.

"Take my word for it," he said, looking a little annoyed.

"Well, are they sweet?" she asked, laughing.

"Yeah, they sweet, baby, but I guess they're naturally sweetened."

"Miles, if those cough drops got any sugar in them, one of these days your fingers and toes are going to fall off and you're not going to have nothing but nubs in their place, because diabetes don't play."

Miles looked at Margaret in amazement, then he spat the cough drops into a bowl on his glass coffee table. "Damn," he said, "you don't ever give a motherfucka a break, do you?" Then he smiled, a big half-moon grin splitting his midnight face.

Moments like these endeared Miles to my family and transformed the celebrated legend into a human being and friend. We loved it, and him—and he loved it, and us. There were many such instances of warmth and closeness during the time I knew Miles, like the fashion shows he would put on late at night to delay me—or Margaret and me—from leaving his place. He would pull out those great outfits he had in his closet and model them for us, strutting around in all his splendor. One night he gave Margaret a marvelous suit and said that he was sorry that he didn't have anything that would fit me because I was too big, which was true.

Sometimes he wanted us to stay because he was lonely. He didn't have that many friends he could just relax with. I remember one night after his video for *Tutu* was previewed at a private club down on Prince Street in New York's Soho district. It was directed by Spike Lee, and all kinds of celebrities turned out for this occasion, including Richard Gere, Walter Yetnikoff (the CEO of Sony and Columbia Records), the singers Ashford and Simpson, Wesley Snipes, and, of course, Spike Lee. Stretch limos lined the narrow street. Champagne was flowing and great food was everywhere. Beautiful women and handsome men trying to look "cooler" than Miles swarmed all over the place. But no matter how hip they thought they were, if they didn't know Miles they were too much in awe, or too afraid, to introduce themselves and speak to him. They watched him from a distance like beautiful mannequins in a Bloomingdale's display window, smiling all the while, and drinking and "stuffing their faces" with all that expensive, catered food.

After a while, Margaret and I got bored with all the stylin' and profilin'. We told Miles we were leaving; it was too plastic for us. He was bored, too, so he left with us, leaving his limousine there. Everyone was shocked. When we got outside, a waiter who worked across the street at Raoul's, a great French restaurant that Margaret and I frequented, was outside. This waiter was also a photographer and he asked me if Miles would mind him taking a photo. I asked Miles and he said he wouldn't mind, so a couple of pictures were taken, one of which still hangs over the entrance into the kitchen and garden in Raoul's restaurant. When we drove uptown, Miles asked us to come up and have some food or something, but we declined. When he got out of the car, he looked hurt that we hadn't taken him up on the invitation. "Later," he said as he walked away from the car and through the doors of his apartment building. I think that was the night I first realized how lonely he often was. On the drive uptown, I remember, Margaret and I talked about how bad we felt because we hadn't hung out with Miles. But it was late, and we both had a lot of stuff to do the next day and we needed to get some sleep. We would have been there until the early hours of the morning, eating, listening to music, watching films, and checking out the "terrible rags" he would have modeled for us.

sending our regrets

The *Tutu* video party reminds me of the annual birthday parties that Miles would throw for himself and a few friends at some great restaurant in Los Angeles or New York, depending on where he was on May 26. A lot of stars came to these parties, like Bill Cosby and his wife, Quincy Jones, Prince, Jasmine Guy, and Lionel Ritchie. Everybody would sit around the birthday table trying to appear cooler than the next person, too hip to even talk to each other. These stars seemed so empty and superficial to Margaret and me. Their lives seemed devoid of passion. So rich and famous and talented, they appeared to be enchanted by themselves, their notoriety, their privilege. So isolated. So detached. So unreal. Partying with the stars was definitely weird.

So in 1990, when we were living in New York, we decided not to attend the next-to-last birthday party that was held out in Los Angeles. Instead, we sent a friend, Teresa Sanchez-Gordon (now *Judge* Sanchez-Gordon), and her daughter, Maya-Luz, with a huge bouquet of flowers. After the maitre d' told him who the flowers were from, our friends were able to carry them in to give to Miles personally. Now, both these women are extremely beautiful, as fine as they come. So when they brought the flowers in to Miles with big grins on their faces, he kept looking at them so hard they got a little nervous. They told me Miles' eyeballs almost fell on the table, he was so amazed. He liked them so much that he invited them to his party, and when they declined, he got up and walked them to the door.

The next day he called me and asked where I was, and how come I hadn't come. I told him I didn't like those kind of affairs because I found them boring. After agreeing, he asked me, laughing all the while, about my beautiful friend and her gorgeous daughter, saying with a deep chuckle of appreciation, "Man, they were finer than a motherfucka." With that I agreed. The following year, in New York (the last year of his life), when he chartered a boat for his birthday party, he didn't even bother asking us to come because he knew we would turn him down, but we did send birthday greetings.

Around this time Miles got real tight with the pop star Prince and started going out to Minneapolis to play and hang out with him. He loved Prince's music and his attitude, and the young star idolized Miles. They had been talking about doing a record together ever since I began writing Miles' book. Somehow it never happened, even though Prince submitted some songs for one of Miles' albums that didn't work out.

Something else that never worked out was that I was never able to arrange for Miles to meet our homeboy Chuck Berry. I wanted to see that happen real bad. They were born in the same year and had never met. I thought it would have been very interesting to get these two innovative musicians and creative spirits together in the same room, turn on a tape recorder, and see what would happen. I knew that a conversation between these two iconoclastic musical titans couldn't have been anything but fascinating. Although Miles said he was willing, it never came about.

strange times

Miles was very loyal to his friends. There are countless stories about him trying to help people he knew from behind the scenes. When James Brown had his run-in with the law and was jailed down in Georgia, I remember Miles trying to find a way to get him out of jail. Since it was not a question of money, Miles tried to figure out if he had any political connections who might help Brown. Finally, he had to realize that he could do nothing.

Then, there was the awful mess my oldest son, Quincy Brandon, found himself in. In his senior year at the State University of New York at Stonybrook, he was falsely accused of raping a white woman and was jailed. Miles' lawyer (and the executor of his estate), Peter Schukat, read about Brandon's situation in the local Long Island paper. Concerned and unable to reach us in the pandemonium—our phone was busy constantly after the news broke—he called Miles, who was touring in Japan and China. One night around four in the morning, the phone rang and woke us out of a dead sleep. It was Miles. After asking how Margaret, I, and Porter were, he got straight to the point, telling me he had heard what had happened to Quincy Brandon and that if I needed anything, to get in touch with Peter, who would do what he could to help. Luckily, we didn't have to—after a long ordeal, everything worked out for Brandon. Still, we never forgot Miles' concern for our family.

Sometime in 1990 I became aware that Quincy Jones wanted to arrange and conduct some of the music Miles had recorded with Gil Evans in the late 1950s. He wanted Miles to play that music live with a big band, perhaps at the Montreux Jazz Festival. At first, Miles hated the idea. He absolutely rejected it and kept complaining about it to me. He loved Quincy as a person and wanted to work with him in some way BUT on some other project—one in which they would create some *new* music. But Quincy persisted and after a while won Miles over. It was all set. They agreed to do it at Montreux, the summer of 1991, and it would be filmed and recorded.

When Miles told me he was going to do it, I tried to tease him in a good-natured way about the fact that he had said he would "never play that old music again," that he would rather die than do so. I told him that he "must be dying," since he was playing his old music. First I saw his eyes flash anger, and then they bore into my eyes like electric screwdrivers. He had never been this angry with me before. I remember wondering, Is he going to hit me?

"Man, *fuck you!*" he said, so fiercely it almost took my breath away, his voice trembling with rage. "What the fuck do *you* know about it? Sheeet. You don't know nothing. You ain't no motherfuckin' musician. You just a writer. What do you know about it? So just shut the fuck up!"

"Hey, man, I was just kidding," I said. "You can play whatever you want to. But it was *you*—not me—that said that you'd 'rather die than play that old shit.' That's what *you* said!"

"Man, fuck you," he said, taking a step forward toward me. "Get outta my house. Right now."

He was livid, his face flushed, spit coming out the side of his mouth. I had never seen him this mad before. He was almost crazed. I started backing up, saying, "Miles, don't think you can hit me and get away with it."

Then, going on the offensive, ready to stand my ground, I got mad, too. "I don't take no ass-whippings, so don't even think about it."

"Get out, motherfucka," he said, almost spitting the words. "Just get outta my house, you hear me? Right now."

"Don't worry, I'm leaving, " I said, backing up toward the door, not trusting him not to hit me in the back of the head if I turned around. No. I wasn't going to expose my back to this crazy man. No way.

"Just leave," he kept saying. "Just leave. Right now."

After I left, he slammed the door so hard I thought he had broken the door frame. I couldn't figure out why he had gotten so angry. I really had been joking, pulling his leg as we so often did with each other, just teasing him. But he had literally exploded with rage. It was the angriest I had ever seen him.

Actually, there was one other equally strange time when he became enraged with me. This happened when we were still working together on the book and one day he convinced himself that I was dating Jo Gelbard just because she and I left Los Angeles for New York on the same day, even though we took different flights. That time, he called New York from Malibu to scream at me to send back a drawing Jo had made of him that he planned to use on the cover of *Amandla*. (It had been my idea to superimpose his image over a map of Africa for the cover, which is what was eventually done.) I had the drawing with me because I wanted to make a photo of it to use in our book.

"Send it back," he kept screaming. "I trusted you like a brother and you stabbed me in my back. You thief. Send it back. Right now! Send back Jo's drawin' of me and that map of Africa. Send it back now!" Then he hung up on me.

Not knowing what this tirade was all about—since we had both agreed that I should take the drawing—I called him right back and said, "Don't hang up on me. I don't know what you're talking about. Stole what? What did I steal? You gave the drawing to me!"

"Just send it back, motherfucka. That's all. Just send it back. Now!"

Then he hung up the phone again. I was livid. If we had been in the same room, there is no telling what I would have done to him. So I picked up the phone and called him again. When he heard my voice, he hung up the phone again. I was defeated and fuming with rage. Later, Margaret called him, and he talked to her, said he didn't want to talk to me. He told her the same thing. "Tell him to send back my fucking drawing and map." Then he hung up on her. So I sent him back Jo's drawing and the map. A few days later, Jo called me and told me why he had been so angry. Miles had thought we were sneaking around with each other. After she reassured him that wasn't happening, he finally called and we talked as if nothing had happened.

This was also what he did after he got so mad at me for teasing him about him playing his old music at Montreux. He just shined it on. About three weeks after our argument, he called and acted just as if nothing had happened. Later, I figured out that maybe the reason he got so angry was because I had hinted at the possibility that he was dying—he *did* die later that year, and he may have had a premonition that he didn't want to be reminded of. That question remains a mystery to me until this very day.

In both cases, he never mentioned the argument again. He never said he was sorry—he was incapable of apologizing, ever, at least in my relationship with him—but he would just act like nothing had happened. Perhaps in his mind, nothing out of the ordinary *had* happened. Perhaps he thought that very angry disagreements were just part of having a relationship. People speak their minds, at times harshly. That's the way life is, or at least that's the way *he* was. After it was over, it was over, and you just went on with your life.

Still, I always thought it strange to have such intense arguments with someone whose music had always given me great pleasure and joy. Miles' music had been the place where I always retreated to when I needed solace or to be energized. His music was, and is today, my safe harbor.

three

listening to miles

"donna" on the jukebox

I entered the world of jazz through a Miles Davis record I heard back in 1955, when I was fifteen years old. I had gone into a fish joint—on Fair Avenue in my hometown, St. Louis, Missouri—to get a jack-salmon fish sandwich (actually a kind of whiting that St. Louis blacks called "jack-salmon"). It could have been a a summer weekday or a Saturday during the school year. I don't remember. All I recall now of walking into that small, nondescript place, since destroyed by so-called urban renewal, is that it was daytime and the sun was shining.

The joint had a yellow linoleum floor and the prefabricated look of vinyl and plastic that later became so popular at McDonalds, Jack in the Box, and all the other banal fast-food restaurants that swept over America and inundate our culture today. Back then, this fish joint was cutting edge, even though the black people in the neighborhood hated the way it looked. We called its sterile style "clean looking," to distinguish it from the usual "greasy spoon" style that most local black eateries wore back then. As we liked to say, this joint was "trying to look white." But we loved the great food that was served up there, and we came back time and again despite our reservations about their "fried hair" and "white look."

Once inside, I immediately noticed a booth filled with four black, hip-looking older guys wearing the latest "in" clothes. Smoking cigarettes and wearing shades, their wide-brimmed hats hanging majestically on the prongs of two steel poles, which seemed to grow beside their booth like facing trees.

The men were sitting there talking and eating deep-fried "jack-salmon" sandwiches doused with hot sauce, with sides of potato salad and cole slaw. They were also listening to the jukebox that was jamming sounds I had either never heard before or never paid attention to. Whatever it was, it was new to me, and at that moment, I was drawn to it like the rabbit to the tarbaby.

I remember being struck by the music easing out of the brightly colored jukebox, which seemed to match the cool style of the four men sitting there nodding their heads in time with the rhythm. In unison. Although I had intended to buy a takeout sandwich, I decided instead to sit down in a booth to eat and listen to those men talk, and to drink in the music they were nodding their heads to.

They talked about the sounds they were hearing on the box. One man said the trumpet was played by a "homeboy" from across the river, someone named Miles Davis. Another said the tune was called "Donna." I also recall one of them saying that "the young alto player sounds almost like Bird. Man, he's something else." Well, I didn't know who Miles was, or "Bird," or the young alto player who sounded like him, either, but I found the conversation fascinating and I listened intently while they played the record over and over again. Jazz music made sense to me that day for the first time in my life.

Until then, my choice in music had always been black rhythm and blues, music I could move my body to—though I suspected that I could also move my body to "Donna," the same way those hip guys were dancing on their hind parts in that booth, nodding their "processed" heads. At that time, I liked the Platters, the Dells, the Cadillacs, Sam Cooke, Johnny Ace, Clyde McPhatter, Jackie Wilson, and the alleged wild man of music who was then living right down the street from me, Chuck Berry. But this music was totally different. It had no words, no voices, no vocal dancing to slide words around, over, ahead, behind, and still land right back on the beat.

It was a completely different kind of music and, after the four men left, I found myself getting up, reaching into my pocket for a nickel, and walking up to the jukebox. I found "Donna," dropped my coin in, turned around, and eased my way back to my booth as the music poured out of the box. As I polished off my second fish sandwich, I kept nodding my head to the tune's insinuating rhythms and moving my hind parts in time to the beat.

becoming hip

When I left that joint that afternoon, I felt as though I had undergone a secret initiation, a rite of passage, one that would separate me forever from the rest of the students who attended Beaumont High School, to which I had just transferred. The school was overwhelmingly white and the students there were "square" to the bone. To my way of thinking, hardly anyone there had any sense of style at all.

During the summer of 1954 my mother had moved us from our old black neighborhood. She had wanted us to be the first black family on the block, but actually we were the second. We were a family of six: my grandmother, Leona Smith; my mother, Dorothy Smith Troupe Brown; my stepfather, China Brown, blues bass player, leader of his own band, and clothes presser at a large cleaning plant; my uncle Allen, unemployed wino, a gentle, harmless man; and my younger brother, Timothy. Our white neighbors hated all of us immediately.

We lived next door to the first black people on the block: a couple, Thomas and Margaret O' Guin. He was a doorman at a local hotel and she was a homemaker. They were older, more conservative than we were, and had no children, which probably explains why they had never had a problem living on Ashland Street before we arrived. Our family brought not only children but young black men into the neighborhood. After we arrived, the whites on the block began leaving faster than people in a movie house when someone's yelled "Fire." Our white next-door neighbors never spoke to us, not once.

In this hostile racist environment, I was fast learning to hate myself just for being black. Earlier in my life, living in a black neighborhood, I had never felt any self-hatred. In fact, it was the other way around; I was proud of who my father was, and of what our family name meant in the black community. My father, Quincy Trouppe (he added a second "p" to his last name because he liked the way it was pronounced when he played in Cuba, Puerto Rico, and Mexico), was a great star in the old Negro baseball league, and his older brother, James ("Pal"), was a leading black political and labor leader around St. Louis, who had also made a ton of money from real estate and "other" investments. A distant cousin, Ernest Troupe, was a lieutenant on the police force. So, within the St. Louis black community, our name was well known and well respected. But, of course, none of the white people in the new neighborhood knew any of this. To them, we were just a bunch of "niggers."

Naturally, I hated the new block and would walk back to my old neighborhood every chance I could get (a distance of about four miles). When I asked my mother why she had moved us, she simply said it had been in our "best interests." *She*, however, travelled outside the neighborhood to work as a telephone operator every day, just as my stepfather, China, and my grandmother did. But my brother Timmy and I had to go to school with the racist neighborhood kids every day, and they were like a pack of howling, rabid dogs.

During my first two years in my new home, the white kids (mostly boys) called me every vile name they knew. They called me "nigger," "coon," "monkey," "gorilla," "jiggaboo," "shinola," and "boy," to name just a few. We fought on many occasions. With the exception of one Italian kid, Tom Palazolla, who invited me to his home, they hardly ever spoke to me or even looked my way during my ears at Beaumont, except when it came to sports (which is how most whites prefer dealing with black men even today). The entire experience seemed designed to drain me of my racial identity and pride.

That's why Miles Davis and his music came to mean so much to me. The white kids at Beaumont High were into Bill Haley and the Comets and Elvis Presley. But what they *really* loved was Pat Boone's rendition of "Ain't That a Shame." I hated Boone's version of that song, because I had heard the "real thing" by Fats Domino, and I knew that Pat Boone had "borrowed" it from him and become famous singing it because he was a white man. Boone made a career of such "borrowings." He also made a "mint" with his cover of Little Richard's "Tutti Fruity." But my white schoolmates didn't know or care about any of this. They didn't give a flying fuck if Boone was getting over because he was covering black songs. It certainly didn't matter to them that Elvis Presley was doing the same thing. Chuck Berry lived in the neighborhood, but the white kids didn't even know his name, not to mention what a great contribution he was making to American music.

But I knew. I knew the "real deal" and it bothered the hell out of me that these white teenagers didn't even care that they didn't know shit; that they could think of black people as stupid and uncreative while all the while their musical heroes were stealing our songs, music, and language and calling them their own.

When I discovered Miles Davis, I knew I had found something these white squares didn't and couldn't know. I was hip. I wanted to be seen as someone completely different from the squares. And, "quiet as it's kept," I really saw myself apart from *all* my high school classmates, the black students as well as the whites. I had no respect for my black classmates because they had bought into the idea of their own inferiority. They believed that their culture, language, and music were beneath those of their white counterparts. So they tried their best to be as white as they could in their speech, dress, and manners. It sickened me to see my old friends change that way. I refused to change, and I guess that sickened both my black and white classmates because we all quickly drew apart.

What happened to us was sad. But at the time I had no language to explain myself to them, nor they to me. We were mute in our separation and pain. We couldn't explain why we were drifting apart. We only knew that we were and that we were powerless to stop it. But I had Miles Davis in my life, and they didn't, and that's what saved me: his music and his living example of what a black man could be: someone completely independent, amazingly creative, fiercely proud.

As a teenager in the late 1950s, I had few fiercely proud black role models and heroes: Miles Davis, Chuck Berry, Paul Robeson, and my father's older brother, Albert, were at the top of my list. Of these men my Uncle Albert was the only one with whom I had a real personal experience—though Chuck Berry lived three blocks down the street from me and I would see and speak to him on occasion. Uncle Albert taught me firsthand what it meant to be what I later came to know as an "unreconstructed black man." This was a dangerous, lonely, and unrewarding position in which to place oneself. Uncle Albert didn't take anything off anyone—black or white—and the reason my father's family had to leave Dublin, Georgia, during the late 1920s was that Uncle Albert, as a teenager, threatened to kill a white man who had called him a "boy" and a "nigger." He refused to be disrespected, whether by a boss, his friends, or anyone else. As a consequence he kept his self-respect but had a hard time keeping employment and making a living. And although they managed to make a much better living than did Uncle Albert, Chuck Berry, Paul Robeson, and Miles Davis were like that, too.

I began to look for more records by Miles. I found out who "Bird" was by finding Miles Davis' name on some of Charlie Parker's records. In the same way I also found out that the "young alto player" who sounded just like "Bird" was Jackie McLean. I wanted to learn everything I could about Miles Davis. So I started asking some of the older guys about him, which led me to my cousin, Marvin, a very good drummer and everyday criminal and junkie. (He was a junkie so obsessed with getting money to support his large habit that he later broke into his own father's house, my Uncle, James "Pal" Troupe, and stole everything that wasn't tied down.

It was the talk of the family for years.) Marvin—dead now—always liked me. He was always telling me I had "potential." Somewhere around 1955 he turned me on to the album *Bags Groove*, which completely blew my mind because it was so different from "Donna" and all the other music by Miles I had heard until then.

bags groove and hard bop

The title track "Bags Groove," named after the vibraphonist Milt "Bags" Jackson and recorded in 1954, was the first jazz music that went straight to my heart and brain, not to mention my body. It had something in it that just moved me to my core, something way beyond what I expected to experience listening to a jazz tune. I had liked "Donna" a lot—still do—and "Walkin'," the signature tune of the "hard bop" movement, and "Blue 'n' Boogie." But "Bags Groove" had something in it that took me completely outside of myself. Maybe it had something to do with the sense of space Miles created, or maybe it was Thelonious Monk's spare, eccentric piano that unlocked the feeling of wide-openness the tune has always had for me, even now. Whatever it was, I know it affected me like no other song I had ever heard.

Even though I had been moving fast through all of Miles' records I could wrap my ears around, I still wasn't prepared for his wide-open, soaring, lyrical voice on "Bags Groove." I loved Monk's wonderful solo in the middle of the song. I loved Bags's vibe work underneath it all, with Percy Heath walking the hell out of his bass lines. And I loved the way that Miles comes back in that clear, crisp, beautiful tone of his. Man, when I first heard "Bags Groove," I felt I had died and gone to some very hip heaven. I also felt I could dance some very cool steps to this music, and, on a number of occasions, I did. But even more than that, more than making me want to move my body, more than challenging me to think about what sound is all about, "Bags Groove" went straight to my heart. It made me feel older and "cool," on the inside of something new. It confirmed my sense that I was a cut above the group I was hanging with, people who weren't into Miles or jazz. And, to be sure, after a short time I found myself uncomfortable with most of these old friends and moved on, eventually finding a place for myself with an older, more adventurous crowd.

What I didn't know when I first heard "Bags Groove" was that in the fall of 1953, just before recording it, Miles had kicked heroin. I knew about his drug habit from my cousin Marvin and I had even thought it had a positive effect on his playing and was one of the reasons he seemed so cool. I wasn't alone in this opinion. In the early 1950s, many hipsters thought that using heroin was very cool. At that time, heroin was just beginning to work its devastating way into urban communities all over the United States. It wasn't moving only into black communities then. In New York it was moving into the Lower East Side (Jewish and Polish and Russian populations) and the Upper West Side (Irish and Puerto Rican populations). In Chicago, in the fifties, a lot of the junkies were Polish and Slovakian. It was really more of an urban poverty issue than a racial one—unlike the crack epidemic of the 1980s, in which cocaine and crack use did split along racial lines.

The reasons I never got involved with heroin were that I was an athlete and that my cousin Marvin, a junkie himself, advised against it. So, because I respected Marvin and trusted his advice, I never shot up or even sniffed it. Still, deep down, I continued to think that the people using heroin were the hippest people I knew. They were so "clean"—well-dressed—and had such hip, laid-back attitudes. But I didn't know that before Miles recorded "Bags Groove," he had secretly gone to his father's farm in Millstadt, Illinois, to kick his habit. That's why he played so great, because he was drug-free, *really* clean.

a case of hero worship

After I fell in love with "Bags Groove" I redoubled my efforts to find out everything I could about "The Prince of Darkness." I began reading all the magazine articles I could find about Miles. I discovered how he dressed—all decked out in elegant clothes and expensive Italian shoes. I checked out his aloof, disdainful but always—to me—cool attitude. From conversations with older black men who had known him in St. Louis, I discovered how he spoke and behaved, and, after absorbing all of this information about him, my own style soon changed. The way I spoke, stood, walked, and dressed changed. Even the way I "hit on" girls changed so my style would be more in line with the way I imagined my hero did things.

Although I wasn't into Bird's music as much as I was into Miles', because of my love for Miles, I paid attention to the news of Charlie Parker's death in March of 1955. Today, I love Bird's music but, perhaps because I grew up with him, I still prefer Miles.

After I first saw Miles play live, as far as I was concerned, he could do no wrong musically or socially. I had had black sports heroes previously, but Miles was my first black hero beyond the world of sports. His music and the way he presented himself to the world opened up the possibility that I would be able to do anything I could imagine myself doing. His music and his example made me feel special. Free. Able to utilize my own imagination.

Later I would come to know that Miles had had the same effect on the lives of many other people from all over the world. In fact, when I was working on his book with him, I discovered there was a group of men and women of all ages and races who followed him around the world attending his concerts, just to hear how differently he would play at each one. I came across them comparing notes at a concert on Long Island. They knew who *I* was. They knew he had chosen me to pen his life story because they knew *everything* there was to know about the man, and they looked up to me because I was the Chosen One. Told me so. I was completely astonished to discover these people, as was Miles, who had known nothing about them because they knew enough about him to keep their respectful distance.

the first quintet

By the time I graduated from high school and went on to Grambling College in Louisiana, Miles' music had changed. The music he and his first "great quintet" created from 1956 to 1960 became some of the most influential small group jazz ever played. John Coltrane, Paul Chambers, Philly Joe Jones, and Red Garland were the personnel. I remember waiting impatiently for every record the group released. And whenever a new record came out, if it was during summer or a holiday break, I would make a beeline over to Percy Campbell's house, on Labadie in St. Louis, to listen to it. Of all my friends, Percy (now dead, having been stabbed in Oakland in the 1970s) had the best sound system and record collection. *Workin'*, *Steamin'*, *Relaxin'*, *Cookin'*: the albums the quintet released became the musical badges of hipness my friends and I proudly displayed in our conversations. The way we saw it was, if you weren't into Miles and Monk, Dizzy Gillespie, Bird, and Art Blakey and the Jazz Messengers, you weren't into anything.

By the time Miles released *Round Midnight* in 1956, he had added the great alto saxophonist Julian "Cannonball" Adderley to the band. This expansion of the group into a sextet led Miles down even greater musical roads, which fact became evident when he released *Milestones* in 1958. In December of 1958, I caught the sextet live at the Sutherland Lounge in Chicago; it was my second time hearing Miles live, and, like the first time, it proved memorable.

I was home from college on Christmas break and some friends and I drove to Chicago to hear them. I had a ton of fun in Chicago, and the Sutherland Lounge was a much hipper place to listen to music than Peacock Alley had been. It was bigger, the acoustics were better, and it seemed as if the audience paid more attention. I got into the club with a false draft card again, only this time it was easier, probably because my friends and I were older. We were flat-out "clean," with the attitudes to match our hip clothes; aloof, disdainful, and too arrogant for words. We didn't have much money—just enough to get in, buy a few soft drinks, and pay for gas for the trip back home—but we were imitating Miles and that got us over. The music the band played that night was glorious. It was so good it was transcendent.

Of course, Miles' music had changed since the first time I heard him live. He was moving full speed ahead into his modal period, and everyone was really beginning to stretch out, taking long solos. Coltrane was something else that night. He yelped and howled and blew so furiously it seemed as though his life depended on every note. He was just beginning to get into the style that would later become known as "sheets of sound." Cannonball was something else, too, tearing off solos that flew like birds. But it was Miles himself who was the spark, the catalyst that ignited, sparked, and drove everyone else that night. The way I remember him playing that evening, his trumpet seemed to soar above the other instruments like a golden eagle, lyrical, probing, and driving everyone to play beyond themselves. He burned through his solos in that now famous "running" style that he had perfected. Then he switched to the mute on the ballads, tonguing the notes like a passionate lover kissing his woman. He was on top of his instrument. He knew it inside and out, knew what to play and when and where to play it. His mind was sharp and free of drugs, his dress was sartorial splendor. Yes, he was "The Man." I tell you he was something else again, and I left the Sutherland Lounge that night completely blown away.

Album after stunning album was released during this great period from 1956 to 1960, one of the most fertile periods any American musician has ever known. And I listened attentively to them all. Sometime during these years, Miles' legendary hipness merged with his great music and turned him into an almost mythical figure. In 1958 alone, *Milestones, Miles and Monk at Newport, Jazz Track,* and *Porgy and Bess* were released. And the next year, perhaps the most celebrated jazz album of all time, *Kind of Blue,* was released. That album would make the already world-famous trumpet player a legend and become the most talked-about and influential record of its time.

kind of blue

Like *Bags Groove,* the album *Kind of Blue* changed the way I listened to music. This was the third time that Miles taught me how to open my ears. After hearing this album, I found that I needed a sense of openness and open-endedness in the music I listened to. I learned to need space within the structure of the composition. I needed surprise, too, rather than the rigid, tightly wrapped sameness that seemed to be typical of a lot of other musicians. After hearing *Kind of Blue,* I began to accept and understand the idea that a great artist works in many different forms and styles, always searching, always challenging the status quo. That's what

I, and many others, began looking to Miles for, this notion of change. We began to understand that it is alright to move away from the familiar and to evolve into something different. We learned that venturing into the unknown could produce something special, as indeed Miles proved with *Kind of Blue*.

I always had loved Miles' tone and his licks. Now, I also expected him to show me something different every time I heard him, to lead me down a different musical path—preferably one that I knew nothing about. This notion was exhilarating—positively revelatory. It brought me closer to understanding the concept of what freedom for a young black man could be. On *Kind of Blue*, Miles once again led me to a place within myself that would teach me something about who I was, about what I thought greatness in music, art, sports, any endeavor could be. *Kind of Blue* became a barometer, as "Donna" and "Bags Groove" had been before it. Miles was my barometer, and no one else came close, not even my father.

Miles' music and his attitude were beginning to affect *how* I chose to live in the world. I was starting to choose flexibility over rigidity as a *must*—as an essential value. When I considered all the different races, religions, subcultures, and social and political philosophies we have in this country, it began to seem imperative that we learn to respect our differences. It seemed to me then—and today seems even more so—that believing in "this *and* that" wins hands down over "this *or* that," which was then and still is the prevailing philosophy—whites *or* blacks, classical music *or* jazz. I was beginning to understand that we could love it all. The improvisations of jazz along with the fixed, unyielding notation of classical music. Because in the modern world one has to be ready for anything, to have the ability to switch up when confronted with the constantly new situations that a multicultural society presents.

It was Miles Davis and his music, his ever-expanding approach to and embrace of many different styles, that taught me to see the importance of inclusiveness rather than separation. Later, other artists would stretch my inclusive vision even further: Pablo Picasso, Pablo Neruda, Gabriel Garcia Marquez, Aime Césaire, and Derek Walcott, to name a few. But Miles Davis remains the most important model for me, because he was the first to demonstrate that it was alright to court change and strive to be different, that you could constantly reinvent your art and do it artfully, with grace, with the possibility of greatness and integrity. Flexibility, not rigidity: Miles was "The Man" who showed the way for millions like me all over the world.

the "bust"

After hearing *Kind of Blue* in 1959, I began to crave change. I didn't know exactly what I was seeking but I *did* know I wanted and needed change. I knew it was out there, because Miles Davis was out there, playing and living it. So I knew it was possible. By 1959, my friends and I were wearing shades all the time like Miles and the other hipsters. We walked the way we thought he walked, we spoke to women the way we imagined he spoke to them, we stood and dressed just like he did. He was our main man. And in our young minds we were just like him.

So in the autumn of 1959 when word came down to us about Miles' run-in with a white policeman outside of Birdland, in New York, we were, to put it mildly, distressed. This incident made him into more than just a musical hero to us. Because of it he became a social and political icon, one who would help usher us into the riotous, tumultuous 1960s.

According to the news reports, the incident began innocently enough, with Miles walking his friend, the famous white newspaper gossip columnist Dorothy Kilgallen, out of the club to get a cab. Out on the street, Miles encountered a white policeman, who asked him to "move on." Miles refused on the grounds that he wasn't loitering as the policeman had accused him of doing, pointing to his name on the display board outside Birdland's entrance to prove it. The cop wouldn't listen to him and a struggle followed, with Miles getting hit on the head by a second policeman, who had been watching in the shadows. After beating and subduing him, they took Miles to Rikers Island, where he spent the night in jail.

It seems like we knew all of this even before the picture of a bloodied Miles walking out of the jailhouse hit the newsstand. In the photograph, his beautiful, stylish first wife, the black dancer Frances Taylor, was draped over his arm. Miles had a bloody bandage wrapped around his head and blood spattered his expensive Italian sports jacket. Despite his injuries, Miles still looked unbroken. In fact, he looked positively defiant, his eyes flashing rage. This photo was flashed all around the world, in the pages of newspapers everywhere. Naturally, it caused outrage among many of his fans, including me.

This photo and the fact that he had defended himself and seemed willing to fight to the death for his rights only increased my respect and admiration for "The Man." After all, this was just before the beginning of the civil rights movement, and respect as equal citizens was what most black people would soon be fighting for. With that incident, Miles vaulted into the political arena of civil rights. (What timing he always had!)

sketches of spain

In 1960, *Sketches of Spain* was released to universal critical acclaim. Gil Evans, Miles' best friend, served as arranger, making this their third album together. Perhaps because of its strong classical European overtones, the critics loved it almost immediately. On the other hand, my friends and I in St. Louis were baffled when we first heard it because it was such a change and so European in its orientation. Then we fell completely in love with it. *Sketches of Spain* proved to be the biggest-selling album of Miles' career until then. (It was later surpassed by *Bitches Brew*.) Today, it remains the favorite Miles album of millions of people.

Released immediately after *Kind of Blue*, *Sketches of Spain* surpassed anything Miles possibly could have imagined. It turned him into a sex symbol, someone who was pursued by beautiful women from all over the world. People who weren't even jazz fans were talking about his impeccable style and taste. Popular magazines like *Time* ran feature stories about him. He had crossed over from being an idol of black people to being an idol of whites, too.

For a black man in 1960 to achieve this kind of musical success was astonishing. Today, such success can be understood only when compared to the impact that Michael Jackson had twenty-five years later. Miles' *Sketches of Spain* was the first real "crossover" moneymaker.

transitions

After finishing college, I joined the army and traveled to France, where I played basketball on American army and French teams. This took me all over Europe—and everywhere I went I found that numbers of people loved Miles Davis, his music, and his style. He was their hero, too. This surprised me, but it only added to my respect for him.

In France I found myself traveling back and forth between Metz, where I was stationed, and Paris, where my girlfriend lived and where I played basketball. It was in France that I began to write poetry, look at art, and associate with others (both French and American) who were considered "bohemian." I began truly interacting with whites and "intellectuals" for the first time, hanging out until all manner of hours (after the basketball season ended) in dark, smoky clubs in Metz and on the Left Bank of Paris. I became a sponge, absorbing all kinds of artistic and political ideas, and by the time I left Europe in late 1964, I was a changed person.

I returned to the United States at the time of assassinations (John and Robert Kennedy, Medgar Evers, Martin Luther King Jr., Malcolm X), incendiary rhetoric, and shoot-outs between black, Latino, and Native American groups and the police and the FBI. These were the violent manifestations of the deep political and cultural changes that were happening then and are still reverberating today. Another aspect of those changes was the growing acceptance of black music and black musicians by white audiences. Rhythm and blues, renamed "rock and roll," was about to conquer white America.

From the beginning of his career, Miles had wanted to reach a wide, racially diverse musical audience. He always wanted to be cutting edge, but he always wanted to be popular, too. In the early 1960s, his challenge was to accomplish both of these goals without compromising his musical integrity. *Sketches of Spain* had brought him a huge audience, but more American whites than African Americans were listening to it. After its great success, Miles wanted more than ever to reach black Americans, especially young black Americans.

Grown weary of playing old standards, he wanted to return to music that was closer to the roadhouse funk he had grown up with—but he also wanted a contemporary sound.

Miles set out to create a more accessible music, one that combined jazz with elements of rhythm and blues, African modal music, and rock and roll. That's just what he eventually did accomplish, but when he achieved his goal he was both celebrated and ridiculed for his efforts by long-time fans and music critics.

He began by listening to the music that was popular with young people: James Brown, Jimi Hendrix, Sly and the Family Stone. He also listened to Motown, the African-American label out of Detroit's inner city, and he was certainly well aware of the company's phenomenal success. Headed by a black man, Berry Gordy, Motown was releasing all kinds of great "crossover" music, and Americans of all races and ethnicities were listening and dancing to Motown's megahits.

sheets of sound

In 1965, for the first time since I had begun listening to him, I wasn't paying much attention to Miles' new recordings because they seemed out of sync with my musical tastes. When I'd returned to the States, after hearing James Brown's "Papa's Got a Brand New Bag," I was out on the dance floor shaking my booty again like everyone else in America. And though I was dancing my ass off to James Brown, it was the energy and passion of John Coltrane and his group that were moving my soul. Trane's surging "sheets of sound" seemed to transcribe the political outrage of the inner cities into profound music. In his music, I heard the gunfire in the streets, the cries of rage, the urgent need to revolt.

In the 1960s, the great social upheavals the United States was experiencing were significantly altering long-standing racial relationships. That fact, and my own political beliefs and emerging artistic consciousness (helped along by Miles' boundary-shattering music), was pointing me toward a fundamental reassessment of my life.

I had moved to Los Angeles to live in the black community called Watts after the riots there in 1965. I lived in a commune of writers, poets, and artists and met many other creative people from all over the community. I joined the Watts Writers Workshop and began to write poetry every day. The one constant presence in my life was John Coltrane. I listened to him every waking hour, sometimes all day long.

But as much as I was learning to love Trane, Miles remained my idol and role model. From the mid- to late 1960s I had memorized almost all of my favorite solos by both musicians. I used their riffs and licks as a foundation for the rhythms and cadences of my own emerging poetic language. Their horn solos helped me to pull myself away from the sonnets, sestinas, and villanelles I was composing when I first started writing poetry.

I kept trying to imitate the flow and structure of their musical ideas. With Miles I wanted to get something like his floating sound and jabbing, insistent staccato rhythms into my poetic lines. With Trane I wanted to learn how to generate the same kind of energy and passionate intensity that his "sheets of sound" did.

the second quintet

In 1966, I "rediscovered" Miles' music. My ears finally opened to his new sound. By then the second quintet (and sometime sextet) had been working together for two years. It took me so long to hear what they were doing because the music was so difficult and different.

In fact, this band was one of the most liberated I have ever heard—then or since. Hearing that band live was like watching a chameleon go through its changes. Night after night, they never played the same tune the same way. Although they played the standards, they did them with extraordinary harmonies and rhythmic experiments. They freed themselves from all the conventional chord changes. But no matter how much they broke with traditions, they swung. They always swung.

The band members were all much younger than Miles and they led him into newer, more challenging directions. The drummer, the late Tony Williams, was seventeen years old, fresh out of Boston and Jackie McLean's band, when he joined Miles. Many people think he was the most gifted drummer Miles ever had. Herbie Hancock was playing great Bud Powell–influenced piano, Wayne Shorter was Miles' most imaginative saxophonist since Coltrane, and the rock-steady and creative Ron Carter on bass completed the core group.

Influenced by the band's exuberant energy and the great tunes the other musicians were writing—especially those of Shorter, the band's main composer—Miles' approach to the trumpet had changed again. His horn had flown into the stratosphere. He played higher and faster than he ever had before, splintering off notes like wood chips flying out of a wood thrasher. The change was so evident it was almost like hearing a new trumpet player. At a club in L.A. one night I overheard music critic Leonard

Feather marveling at how fast Miles was playing. He kept shaking his head in amazement about Miles' great new sound.

In the few years that the quintet/sextet was together, the personnel and instruments kept changing and electric instruments were added. For Miles, electrical amplification represented the future of music—but it also led to the breakup of his second great band.

in a silent way

The year 1968 was a momentous one for Miles. He began a short-lived marriage to Betty Mabry, he suffered from a depression caused by the death of his friend John Coltrane in 1967, and he found himself searching for a new sound again. As Dizzy Gillespie once said, "Miles is like a man who has made a pact with himself to never repeat himself." And, I, after hearing Miles play the memorable solo "Petits Machins" ("Little Stuff") on the album *Filles de Kilimanjaro,* was altogether into his music again.

With the release of *In a Silent Way,* it was clear that Miles had found his new sound. At first, it was hard to listen to, because I had just recently become accustomed to the second quintet, and I wasn't ready for him to move in another direction; but it wasn't long before I was loving the new sound. By then, I understood that one important reason to love Miles was that you would never know what to expect from him. It wasn't that his playing was so different on *In a Silent Way* but rather that he had placed himself in a new musical context. He had surrounded himself with an entirely new sound that brought his voice into sharp relief, allowing us to hear it in a more open and expanded way. There were deep, mysterious spaces in the music and there was something mysterious and magically compelling beneath its surface that bubbled like an underground river. It drew me back to listen to it over and over again.

In a Silent Way uses three electric pianos, an electric organ, and an electric guitar in addition to conventional acoustic instruments. All the musicians take long solos, but Miles' are especially bright, haunting, and, at their core, sad. Miles had learned and absorbed so many new musical ideas from the members of his second "great" band that he had caught up with the musical language of the younger generation. And once he was comfortable with new instruments like the synthesizer, he felt it was time to move on. He wanted to move forward with his own musical agenda, and he knew he wanted to go in the direction of Jimi Hendrix, James Brown, Sly Stone, and Charles Lloyd. Years later, Miles told me that Charles Lloyd had served as a catalyst for how he had played *In a Silent Way*. Still, though Miles had loved the way Lloyd had fused elements of rock and jazz together, it was not Lloyd but guitarist Jimi Hendrix who was the biggest influence on Miles at this time.

"jimi"

I met Hendrix in California around the same time Miles was introduced to him in New York. I met Hendrix when I was reading poetry on the beach in Venice, but I didn't know who he was because he told me only that his name was "Jimi." He liked my poetry and offered to play behind me, and I accepted. His amazing guitar blew me completely away, so I asked for his full name. When he told it to me, I was so astonished I couldn't read anymore. My mouth dropped down somewhere around my knees and he just stood there laughing at me. Laughing and watching my reaction. He was a shy man and was flattered that I loved his music so much and that I knew who he was, because, as he later told me, most blacks had never heard of him. That was because the kind of music he played appealed mostly to the young white fans of rock and roll.

The following week I came back to Venice to read at the beach and Hendrix was there and played behind me again. That was the last time I ever saw him up close. I didn't know that he knew Miles, nor did I ever mention to him how much I loved Miles' music. But I did find out later that Hendrix had influenced Miles so much that Miles had tried to transpose his guitar style for the trumpet.

bitches brew

Miles had plunged deep into electric instrumentation for the first time on *In a Silent Way,* and he continued in this direction even further with his next album, the ground-breaking *Bitches Brew,* which rose to the top of the jazz charts and eventually sold five hundred thousand copies, becoming Miles' biggest-selling record.

Like *Kind of Blue*, it exerted a tremendous influence throughout the worlds of jazz, pop, rock, and blues.

But more than any other album until then, it polarized his audience into two distinct groups: those who loved his music before *Bitches Brew* and those who loved it after hearing *Bitches Brew*. In the first group were the older lovers of jazz and European classical music, perhaps evenly divided among all racial groups. His new audience was equally diverse but decidedly younger and more tuned into rhythm and blues, rock and roll, and funk. When they came together at Miles' concerts, the two groups were like oil and water; they were loudly contentious and even got into arguments about which way Miles should take his music.

However, it was the younger group that raved about *Bitches Brew* and bought it, and it was on the hook of the younger group that Miles hung his musical hat. One thing is certain: Miles knew exactly what he was doing. He knew that his new approach would reach the younger generation and, like the true innovator that he was, didn't care what anyone else thought. He once told me, "Old people don't buy records but young people do."

He sure was right in this assessment, because many of his older fans never bought a record of his again after *Bitches Brew*, and this included many of my older friends. I think it was a class difference as well as a generational one. His older audience liked to wear suits and ties and go to concert halls. Many of them also liked European classical music and opera. The kids who liked *Bitches Brew* were not only younger; they were raunchier. They dressed down instead of up and danced in the aisles and cheered in the "wrong" places. They were bored by classical music or opera but loved rock and roll, funk, and soul.

I, for one, appreciated Miles' courage, especially because it seemed to me that he was at the top of the music world when he made these changes. In my opinion, it's a lot easier to change when you're closer to the bottom than when you're on top. Miles always initiated change when he was riding high and being richly rewarded for what he was doing. The cause of his many changes was never financial need. It was what he needed to do to advance as an artist.

Others didn't see it that way, especially the critics. After *Bitches Brew*, Stanley Crouch called Miles "the most brilliant sellout in the history of jazz" and a "traitor." Leonard Feather, who had been one of Miles' biggest fans, didn't appreciate the change, either. But then, until a certain point in time, Feather hadn't liked John Coltrane, and he'd urged people not to buy Trane's records or to listen to him live because they would only be listening to "noise." Miles once told me that Feather had urged him not to include Trane in his first great group. Time sure proved him wrong on that point.

Miles went his own way despite the beating he knew he would take from hostile critics and fans. Miles knew that all forms of art reflect their own societies and cultures. In 1969, despite the furious objections of the purists, he knew that electrical instrumentation was here to stay. As Ralph Gleason wrote: "Electric music is the music of this culture and in the breaking away (not the breaking down) from previously assumed forms a new kind of music is emerging. The whole society is like that. The old forms are inadequate. Not the old eternal verities but the old structures." Miles, according to Gleason, was always reaching for "new ideas and new forms, and in music this has meant leaving the traditional forms of bars and scales, keys and chords, and playing something else altogether which maybe you can't identify and classify yet but which you recognize when you hear it and which when it makes it, really makes it—is the true artistic turn-on."

If Miles and his band were excited about what they had accomplished with the recording of *Bitches Brew*, it did not equal the shock that his fans went through when they first heard it—whether they loved it or hated it. The first thing I noticed when I bought the album was the cover. It was truly strange. It was a "cosmic" painting by Abdul Mati of three black people looking at sea and sky, two men and a woman. The woman's hair seems like a small tornado connecting her head to the dark clouds in the sky. She has an arm around a man's waist and he has an arm around her shoulders. They are nude above the waist. Another black face juts out of the left margins above a flaming pink flower. All three seem to be Africans looking westward toward what could be America. This was the first time Miles had used original art on an album cover, and it seemed more suited to a rock album than to jazz. Even the title of the album seemed more in keeping with rock and roll than with jazz, and the cover announced the psychedelic orientation of the music within.

I remember getting ready to listen to the record by fixing myself a stiff drink, going into the front room of my home in Athens—I was teaching at Ohio University at the time—and placing the first of the four sides (*Bitches Brew* is a double album) on the turntable. When the drumbeat opened up the music, I sat down eagerly. It was early afternoon and I kept listening until late into the evening, even bringing my dinner into the front room to eat with my plate on my lap as I absorbed every note and chord of this at first very weird music. Before the night closed down, it had deeply impressed me.

It took a while for me to understand what Miles was doing and to hear the music's roots. *Bitches Brew* went even deeper into the rock-funk-blues bag than had its predecessor, *In a Silent Way*. Yet it is a direct descendent of that album, with its modernist edge and its expansive search for freer modes and ways to express musical ideas.

The album begins with Joe Zawinul's tune "Pharaoh's Dance," which opens in a swirling maelstrom of electrical pulsations that carry the listener into a strange new place where nothing is predictable. Guitars and electric pianos lay out short runs that widen like the concentric circles a rock makes when it is thrown in a river. Then comes Miles' first mournful, very short solo, and after that, when the other musicians start up again, Miles seems to jab and punch his way like a boxer through an enveloping sound that swirls all around him. His horn almost screams a few times as if frustrated at not finding a way out of all that sound. The group mimics the traffic noise of rush hour in Manhattan, with car horns honking and millions of people talking and yelling in a hurricane of voices. It is a remarkable opening. Even today, whenever I think about Manhattan, I think about "Pharaoh's Dance."

The title tune starts slowly. Miles opens with a marchlike, trilling solo that moves into a long passage that rises, falls, and spreads out as if the trumpeter were descending into some kind of private hell. His voice sometimes screams, other times pleads. The trilling, marchlike figure, reminiscent of his drum and bugle beginnings, is repeated throughout the composition like a refrain. Miles' solo in the middle of this twenty-seven-minute piece is stunning in its creation of a feeling of profound loneliness and isolation.

In contrast, "Spanish Key," which opens up the second side of the album, pulsates throughout. It churns and boils like water in an iron cauldron over a large fire. Everyone who solos here does so splendidly—John McLaughlin, Chick Corea, Wayne Shorter, Benny Maupin, Zawinul, and, of course, Miles.

"Miles Runs the Voodoo Down" is a memorable Miles Davis composition. From the opening bass line punctuated by drum accents and guitar blues licks to the bass clarinet moaning in the background of Miles' opening statement, you know this is the blues, but the blues played in a way you've never heard before. The music seems to be boiling, with voices emerging from whatever the concoction is that is being cooked down there. "Sanctuary" closes out this very controversial album more in the style of his second great quintet. When set against the rest of the songs on this album, its haunting tune seems almost tame.

Bitches Brew broke down the barrier between rock and traditional jazz. Some critics, fans, and musicians never forgave Miles for doing this, but he was celebrated by millions for pushing the envelope of innovation and creativity in that direction. The album also pushed Miles into larger venues than the small jazz clubs he had played for years. *Bitches Brew* not only generated controversy; it made Miles richer, too, and more famous than he had ever been. He played gigs with the Grateful Dead, Carlos Santana, and the late Laura Nyro, taking his music to an ever-growing, larger audience.

miles' "stock" bands and recordings

After *Bitches Brew*, Miles drew more and more from the same pool of musicians—his "stock recording band" as he liked to call it—to make his new recordings. This was true for *Circle in the Round*, *Live-Evil*, *Big Fun*, *Get Up with It*, *Jack Johnson*, and *On the Corner*, all recorded in the early 1970s, though some, like *Circle in the Round*, were released much later. *Live-Evil* was an extension of what Miles had done on *Bitches Brew*, using some of the same musical concepts and figures, only this time around, in his words, they were "more worked out" because on *Live-Evil* he knew exactly where he wanted the music to go.

He was moving away from everyone having a solo to using more ensemble interplay and group improvisation, a hallmark of funk and rock. This caused an even larger rift between Miles and the jazz purists because jazz has always been considered the soloist's art form, the place where an individual can improvise and solo to his or her heart's content. Now Miles was moving away from even this sacred tenet. There were still solos, but they were shorter, more intense bursts within the group context. For many of his older fans, this change proved to be the last straw; but their places in Miles' audience were eagerly taken by younger, rock- and funk-oriented fans.

Between 1965 and 1970, Miles released many albums that carried his name as leader. All of them used members of the stock recording band that he had developed over the years. It seemed as though he was living and sleeping in the recording studio. Most of the albums I liked, listening to them over and over again; some I was indifferent to, listening to them only occasionally; others I listened to once and never played again. But if Miles was becoming more prolific during these years, he was also becoming more improvisational when he played live at concerts.

During this period Miles was literally making up the music onstage, creating it as the concert went along. Songs grew longer and longer and he completely abandoned the traditional standards, like "My Funny Valentine" and "If I Were a Bell," that had driven Coltrane out of his band. In 1971, when Miles toured the United States playing rock halls as the opening act for Carlos Santana, many jazz fans and critics were more confused than ever. But even if it didn't appear that way from the outside looking in, Miles knew that he was moving toward the music of *On the Corner*.

on the corner

On the Corner, recorded in the summer of 1972, was released later that year. The critics and fans who had thought *Bitches*

Brew the most controversial jazz album Miles would ever release had more surprises in store, because *On the Corner* was indeed just right around the corner. This album produced more shocked dismay among jazz purists than even *Bitches Brew*. I, too, was confused and disappointed when I first heard it. But I came to think, and still do, that *On the Corner* was a powerfully innovative album.

The album cover—paintings of black street scenes by California artist Corky McCoy—made it clear that Miles was reaching out to young African Americans. I could see that. I knew he was trying to play jazz with a James Brown funk groove. I could hear that. But, as I said, the music confused me at first, because it wasn't James Brown and it wasn't Miles Davis but something else altogether different, with lots of Indian instruments like sitars and tablas thrown into the acoustic and electric mix for good measure.

Initially, I was even disappointed by Corky McCoy's cartoonlike drawings of black people on the cover. But the second time I listened to it and looked at the cover drawings, I heard the rhythm underneath that pulled me into the music, and I understood McCoy's images, too. The album has not let go of me since. *On the Corner* is quintessentially an album that comes from the sounds, rhythms, and attitudes that permeate the culture of that great city, New York.

In 1972 I was living on Manhattan's Upper West Side in a sixteenth-floor apartment on Central Park West with a wonderful view of Central Park. I knew that Miles was living on 77th Street, a block and a half off Broadway. Yes, I was in New York

City and I felt as though I was in heaven. Tall buildings, millions and millions of people, all kinds of cultures and sounds mashed together. Close up.

Had I not been living in New York, perhaps I wouldn't have gotten into *On the Corner* on just my second hearing, but living there made me more receptive and helped me penetrate the music's density and get right down into its rhythmic core.

On the Corner is definitely African-American urban funk tinged with jazz and Indian and African flavors. It's a jambalaya or gumbo from New Orleans. It's "hip-hop" before "hip-hop." Indeed, it might have been the first hip-hop record released by a major label, with its recurring bass and high-hat drum rhythms punctuated by snare accents, its use of electrical instrumentation, and its looping use of the recording tape.

On the Corner is all about an urban musical attitude and its orientation is funk, while its wonderful displays of musicianship are the improvisational skills found in the best of jazz musicians. A deep groove is laid down from jump, a rhythm that bumps and bounces along like a hip black man or woman walking down a New York street and taking in all the sounds and images. You can hear the car horns.

Miles plays wah-wah guitar rhythms on his horn, wailing, screeching, screaming, and meowing like a cat in the night. And though there are fine featured solos, *On the Corner* is really about group ensemble playing. The drummers and percussionists anchor this recording and goose and push it with an unbelievable pulsation and synchronicity. In the background, bells shake, gourds are scratched and shaken, whistles are blown. The drummers make the sock cymbals shimmy and shake like the behinds of men and women bouncing up and down and side to side on Harlem streets. The rhythmic figures are repeated throughout in a hypnotic fashion, but everyone is part and parcel of the ensemble group sound that percolates and brews and boils and spills over everything.

With this record, Miles proved definitively his ability to absorb different musical genres and turn them into his own musical idiom. *On the Corner* is a great synthesis. Over time I have grown to cherish it as much as I do any other album Miles ever made. In my opinion, it is a masterpiece that captures the music and sounds and feeling of our times like no other. Of course, the purist jazz critics hated it and had a field day bad-mouthing it, but it was not only panned by mainstream jazz critics—it didn't sell well, either. Initially, then, it sank like a stone. But time has done well by it because as many young music lovers have discovered it, it has become an indispensable record for them.

On the Corner was a harbinger for the direction Miles would take from 1972 until 1975, when bad health, cocaine addiction, alcoholism, and disinterest in what he was playing—and with the entire music scene—forced him into five years of silence. From 1975 until 1980, he did not play a concert, cut a record, or even pick up his horn to practice. He just slid further down into drug and alcohol addiction, sex orgies, and a lifestyle that kept him prowling the streets of Manhattan during the hours after midnight like a madman or predator.

backstage at avery fisher

The last time I heard Miles play live before he retired was at the Kool Jazz Festival at the Avery Fisher Hall. It was a great and strange night. I went to the concert with my homeboy and friend pianist John Hicks and another friend, writer Steve Cannon. Hicks had told me that Miles had asked him to play at the concert, so he had gotten us great balcony seats overlooking the stage, and backstage passes so we could hang out with Miles and the musicians after the concert. Hicks was overjoyed to be playing with Miles, and I was happy for him and for the opportunity to be there to celebrate with him. After all, he was one of the guys who used to sit up in the bleachers at Tandy Community Center back in St. Louis and say—along with me and some other guys—that he was going to "run away to New York City and be just like Miles Davis." So here we were, hanging in New York City, chilling, with me thinking I was finally just about to meet Miles. I remember thinking that it just couldn't get any better than this.

When the band took the stage I saw that the working band had changed again—this time Miles was on trumpet and on the electric organ and keyboards. Sonny Fortune was on saxophones, Pete Cosey and Reggie Lucas on electric guitars, Michael Henderson on electric bass, Al Foster on drums, and Mtume on percussion. But no John Hicks. Where was he? I thought that he would probably come out in a short while, but he didn't. It was very strange. He didn't join us in the extra seat we had, either. I remember thinking he would show up sooner or later.

The concert was great, one that brought people to their feet many times with whistling and standing ovations. Miles was playing with fire that night. The rest of the group played what music critic Howard Mandel later called "scorched earth music," saying they were "burning the house down" with their music that night. Music critic Greg Tate called that band "the world's first fully improvisational acid-funk band." And it was that, too. I also remember the crowd being younger and blacker than previous ones, but with lots of Latinos, whites, and Asians, too. It was certainly a more multicultural audience than any I had ever seen at Miles' concerts in the past.

When the concert was over, Steve and I went backstage to see if we could catch up with John Hicks. We found him standing just outside Miles' dressing room door, ranting and raving, madder than a motherfucker. When he finally calmed down he told us that Miles had been so high he had forgotten that he had asked Hicks to play. Miles told Hicks that he, Miles, was going to play piano that night, which he did. Well, that just about sent Hicks off the deep end, and he threatened to hit Miles upside his head with a beer bottle; but some of the musicians stepped in, stopped him, and cooled the whole thing out. When we were leaving, Hicks said it was the drugs that were making Miles trip that way.

The energy backstage that night after that concert was awful. I had never seen Hicks so angry—and I had known him for twenty years. He was always smiling, even while playing some of the "baddest" piano around. I remember feeling very bad and sad for him when we left the hall that night to get ourselves a stiff drink. I also remember thinking that Miles couldn't keep going on like that, being so fucked up on drugs that he would forget something as important as who he had asked to play with him at a concert. John Hicks wasn't a liar; he took his music and everyone else's seriously. So I knew the problem had to be with Miles, and that disturbed me. It also disturbed me that he could do such a hurting thing to so fine a musician. My respect for Miles slipped that night. I remember thinking that just because someone was a legend, that didn't give him the right to treat a person as badly as Miles had treated John Hicks. It was awful. A year later, in the summer of 1975, Miles retired from the music scene, and he didn't come back for five long years, leaving a big hole in the music and in many of our lives.

miles points the way

Miles' New York comeback concert, on July 5, 1981, again at Avery Fisher Hall, during George Wein's Newport Jazz Festival, was a huge musical and media event. He had already played Boston's Kix Club on June 27 to packed crowds, but Boston isn't New York City and on July 5 a host of important music critics and celebrities like Bill Cosby, Mick Jagger, Dustin Hoffman, Quincy Jones, Clint Eastwood, Elizabeth Taylor, Woody Allen, and Richard Gere turned out to greet and hear Miles. A slew of great musicians, like Max Roach, Clark Terry, Jackie McLean, Ornette Coleman, Jack DeJonette, Wynton and Branford Marsalis, Sonny

Rollins, Art Blakey, Abbey Lincoln, Mtume, the late Jules Hemphill, and Dizzy Gillespie, also were in attendance, along with many, many others.

I was there, too, along with my future wife, Margaret. Everyone was "dressed to kill." And although his comeback album, *The Man with a Horn* (1980), had been totally savaged by the critics (I too was deeply disappointed with the music on this album), everyone was there to hear what Miles was now into musically, since its release had been some months earlier. In the end most went away happy, because the music was popping—even though Miles' trumpet chops still weren't all the way back, his musical ideas were almost there. Still, his playing was much better and stronger than it had been on *The Man with a Horn*, where it had been dismal. He sounded much better, richer, more adventurous in his playing, and this encouraged almost every Miles fan there. His band that evening was first-rate: Marcus Miller on electric bass, Mike Stern on guitar, Bill Evans on saxophone, Al Foster on drums, and Mino Cinelu on percussion, with his guest artist for the evening the beautiful and outstanding percussionist Sheila E.

His fans' encouragement was rewarded with his playing on his next album, *We Want Miles*, which is a compilation of Miles' 1981 summer concerts at Kix and Avery Fisher Hall and his September tour of Japan. By his Japanese tour there is a marked improvement in Miles' playing over what I heard in July at Avery Fisher Hall; his sound, tone, and attack are much richer, stronger, and more confident. *We Want Miles* sold over a hundred thousand copies (extremely well for a jazz album) and won a Grammy—a "sympathy vote," I remember one of his detractors saying after the award was announced. I didn't think so, because there were some very nice cuts on that album, including "Back Seat Betty," "Jean-Pierre," and "Fast Track," all composed by Miles.

By the time his next album, *Star People*, was released in 1982, his playing chops were even better. And although I liked this album—especially "Speak," "It Gets Better," and the blues tune "Star People"—it was his next album, *Decoy* (1984), that fully got my attention. Even though it was awarded the Grammy for that year, I don't think it's one of his greatest albums, although it includes some good tracks, notably the title tune, "Code M.D." (for "Miles Davis"), "Freaky Deaky," 'What It Is" (a favorite expression Miles used when greeting friends with one of his rare smiles), and "That's Right." The music on this album is open, airy but tight, and very, very rhythmic, with catchy contemporary musical hooks, funk grooves, and a group sound so large it seems like a big band is playing in many places.

Miles' next album, *You're Under Arrest*, also sold over a hundred thousand copies, in a very few weeks. This was due in part, in my opinion, to Miles including the very popular songs "Human Nature" and "Time After Time" on this album, tunes that would remain in his live performance repertoire until his death. Again, this wasn't one of my favorite albums, though it had some moments, like those two lovely pop ballads, the opening track entitled "One Phone Call Street Scene" (which features Miles, Sting, and others talking), "Intro M D 1," and "Katia" (two other songs he kept in his concert repertoire).

Miles said he made this album because of "the problems that black people have with policemen everywhere." He personalized this belief when he said: "The police are always fucking with me when I drive around out in California. They didn't like seeing me driving around in a sixty-thousand-dollar yellow Ferrari, which I was doing at the time I made this record. Plus, they didn't like me, a black person, living in a beachfront house in Malibu. That's where the concept for *You're Under Arrest* came from." Miles sometimes drove around with an expired license and old Georgia plates, but his logic was, "The police know who I am, so why do they have to stop me?"

Still, the arresting part of this album—at least for me—is the striking photo of Miles on the cover and back of the album. He's dressed in all black, with a wide-brimmed black hat and a no-nonsense look on his face, and is holding what looks like an automatic rifle. It's a stunning photograph.

The good thing I would say about this album is that Miles plays very well here; his sound and tone are bright and clear, his playing and attack are very confident, very strong. Throughout this album he shoots off flying riffs in high and middle registers with ease—his playing chops are fully back!—and he has perfected the big-band sound that will remain a signature of his band until his death.

I liked the huge sound, the way it was structured, layered, and arranged, the way each musical instrument was voiced. Miles had learned much from Duke Ellington, Stockhausen, and Paul Buckmaster about using rhythm and space, about how to manipulate the band's sound from high to low and all points in between, in the blink of an eye. Among the modern jazz musicians he was, in my opinion, unsurpassed in achieving this huge, layered big-band sound with relatively few—six or seven—musicians. *You're Under Arrest* was the last album Miles recorded for Columbia Records, ending what had been a very rewarding recording relationship of almost thirty years.

Miles moved over to Warner Records, and on his first album, *Tutu,* named after South Africa's black Nobel Peace Prize laureate Bishop Desmond Tutu, he reaches the highest plateau with his layered "big-band" sound. From the opening track, "Tutu," on, Miles' manipulation of the band's sound is masterful. For me this is the most completely rewarding of his final albums—although I truly like *Amandla, Aura,* and *Live Around the World.* All of these albums are rich and nourishing, and in different ways.

Aura is outstanding for its inventive, adventurous spirit and structure. Recorded in 1984 in Copenhagen, in collaboration with the remarkable Danish composer and trumpet player Palle Mikkelborg, this record was released by Columbia (because Miles was under contract with them when it was recorded) in 1989. The album has a wonderful experimental edge to it, both in its compositional structure—all by Mikkelborg—and in the musicianship on display here.

Miles' playing on this album is really outstanding. His solo riffs at times soar into the stratosphere. On other occasions, he plays a more thoughtful horn, open or muted, his solos sometimes long and sometimes fragmented, seemingly bitten off just as they get started. On still other occasions he plays with a pure introspective beauty reminiscent of his earlier, pre-electric phase. All in all, it is a wonderful album.

Amandla (meaning "freedom" in Swahili) is also a truly first-rate album, continuing the layered big-band sound, only funkier. The album has more of a Caribbean and African touch because Miles was really listening to Kassav and zouk and Franco, the late great Zarian guitarist. (I know because, as the reader will recall, I introduced Miles to their music.) *Amandla* has splashes of guitar and synthesizer colors patched into the group sound that echo Kassav's wide use of the guitar, electric bass, and synthesizer. It's a subtle effect, but it's there underneath it all.

Live Around the World is rewarding for other reasons, mainly because it captures how really magnificent Miles' last bands were live and in concert.

Although very, very interesting in places, *doo-bop*—like Ralph Ellison's last novel, *Juneteenth*, published in June 1999—is an unfinished project, because Miles died before the album could be completed. Had he lived, I am convinced, *doo-bop* would have been more fully realized, and possibly the innovative, truly outstanding record that Miles told me he wanted to make. As is, *doo-bop* is only an indication, a musical index finger, if you will, pointing in the direction music might go in the future. Already some musicians, like Branford Marsalis, Greg Osby, and Russell Gunn, have released intriguing musical albums that move confidently in that direction, and perhaps beyond.

i see things

When I listen to Miles play I see things. I hear birds sing. I see and hear rivers and midnight trains as they cross a lonely midnight, midwestern landscape. I see beautiful women floating, naked and clothed; I see stylish men, pimps and slick-dressing gangsters. See ghosts all up in and between his chords, and I hear old and young people talking on southern porches after the sun has gone down. I hear horses whinnying and dogs barking. I mean, the way his sound flows is, for me, like seeing a parade of very hip people, magical in their elegance, flow by in an unending stream of eloquence just as the sun sets in the west and all those marvelous colors are singing their sundown song. He was magical for me when I first heard him and he was magical at the end, and he still is. Not despite all the changes in style his music and playing went through, but because of them.

four

saying good-bye

When Miles Davis died on September 28, 1991, in Santa Monica, California, of heart failure brought on by diabetes and pneumonia, he died in Jo Gelbard's arms. Jo's mother, Iris Kaplan, also a painter, told me this when Margaret and I had dinner with her and her husband, Lenny, a few months after Miles' death. Iris told me that Jo had sensed he was going and just climbed into bed with him right before the end.

Just like that, he was gone. All that fierce energy, all that light and all that darkness. Gone. Just like that. A stroke paralyzed him, put him in the hospital. Then a second stroke killed him. (His father had died of a sudden stroke, and in the summer of 1996, his oldest sister, Dorothy, would die of stroke, too, so they seem to run in the family.) The official cause of death was given as pneumonia and, I think, heart failure.

Margaret told me that Miles had had a stroke when she met

me at the San Diego airport in the first or second week of September. Dorothy, Miles' sister, had just called to let me know and had asked her to have me call when I arrived. I had just talked to Miles on the phone earlier that week from Minneapolis, where I was spending a month as writer in residence at The Loft. We had talked about meeting the following week to begin outlining plans to collaborate on a musical we had been discussing. So when Margaret told me the bad news, I was shocked. I called Dorothy right away and she told me it wasn't looking good for Miles, that he was paralyzed on his right side, that he was hooked up to all kinds of tubes, and that he was unconscious. "Are you coming up to see him?" she wanted to know. If I was, she would arrange a pass for me to get into the hospital.

I thought about it for a while and told her, "No, I'm not coming. I want to remember him like he was the last time I saw him." I told her I didn't want to see him lying up there helpless, with tubes running all up into him, up his nose. Told her I wanted to remember him—selfish as this might sound—alive, full of great energy, with that fierce attitude about him, told her I couldn't bear seeing him helpless. I told her that I just couldn't take that, that I was sorry, which I was. (A few years later, Ricky Wellman, Miles' last drummer, told me he *had* gone to see Miles right before he passed and was shocked by the image of him lying there inert, seemingly waiting for death. Ricky said he found himself wishing sometimes he hadn't seen Miles in this way, because this image seemed to dominate all the rest of the remembrances he had of Miles.)

Dorothy said she understood, that the family was there and that

Clark Terry, Miles' boyhood idol and old friend, was calling every day. She said that although he was unconscious, he would move his left hand ever so slightly every time he heard Clark Terry's voice. I thought it was wonderful that Clark was calling Miles. It seemed that Miles had come full circle and was depending on his old friend again for emotional sustenance.

I was in Statesboro, Georgia, when Miles passed. I had gone there as the last stop on a ten-city poetry tour of the state. I found out about Miles' death from the television when I came back to my hotel room in Statesboro. I saw his face flash on CNN and started to realize that he was gone. Although after talking to Dorothy I had known that he probably wouldn't make it, his death still stunned me and left a hole in my heart. I loved the man, no matter what.

Miles' death was peaceful and, considering the condition he was in, probably for the best. Had he survived, he would have been paralyzed and most likely bedridden for life. He would have been unable to play ever again and probably would have gone crazy in that condition. It would have been pure torture. Yes, I think under the circumstances, it's best that he died and did not have to live as an invalid. He would have hated that.

After his death, I began to think that he *knew* he was dying, and perhaps that was why he got so angry with me when I reminded him that he had said he would rather die before he "played that old-time music again." If he felt himself dying, maybe he thought that I had peeped his hold card. I don't know. I *do* know that the last time I saw him he seemed weaker than he had ever seemed before.

Miles never talked about death; he even hated the subject being brought up. He hated going to funerals, too. In 1987, when I told him that James Baldwin had died, he hadn't heard the news yet and couldn't seem to get it together in his head that Jimmy was gone. They had been long-time friends, and Jimmy's place in St. Paul de Vence in southern France was the only friend's home I knew about that Miles stayed at when he was traveling.

After hearing of Jimmy's death, Miles kept saying that he had just seen him earlier in the year when he had played France. He had known that Jimmy was sick but was convinced that of all his friends, Jimmy would outlive him. I thought I saw tears in his eyes, but if there were, Miles covered them up well by excusing himself and going into the bathroom. One thing was certain: Miles Davis wasn't going to let me or anyone else see him cry. But I think on that cold December day in 1987 Miles Davis did cry for his great friend. He stayed in the bathroom for quite a while and when he came out there was no sign of tears, though his eyes were red and he was sniffing and blowing his nose into a handkerchief. "Man," I remember thinking to myself, "Miles is one tough, thick-skinned motherfucka."

After I asked him if he was going to attend Baldwin's funeral, he said, "I ain't going to no funeral. I don't like no goddamn funerals, even if it is Jimmy Baldwin's. I want to remember him in life, in the flesh, when he was livin' and was a bad motherfucka and not some ghost of himself layin' up in no coffin. That ain't Jimmy," he said in his hoarse whisper of a voice, "but just a pile of lifeless flesh and bones. Naw, man, I want to remember him how he was: a bad motherfucka. That's all." (That's why I didn't visit Miles in the hospital or go to his funeral; I wanted to remember *him* as the "bad motherfucka" he was.)

Throughout that day he talked about many of his friends who had died—Monk, Bird, Coltrane, Fats Navarro, Freddie Webster, Bud Powell, Red Garland, Jimi Hendrix, Clifford Brown, and many, many others. But he talked about his old drummer, Philly Joe Jones, the most, shaking his head and chuckling to himself every time he mentioned Philly Joe's name. Miles didn't laugh; he kind of chuckled, sometimes emitting a raspy, throaty shaking. It was clear that Miles had loved Philly Joe, and that day it was also clear that Miles had loved James Baldwin deeply.

That conversation was one of the rare times I heard Miles talk about death. That day I realized that Miles had lost many great friends; that with the exception of Dizzy Gillespie (who would die soon after Miles), Max Roach, Clark Terry, and a few others, Miles was almost the last of the beboppers.

Miles believed in the spirit, in life after death, and the last time I saw him—at his new Central Park West address, in the summer of 1991—he was talking about death. Maybe he knew that his time was coming, felt it in his body, or maybe his doctors had told him he didn't have long. Miles talked about how he missed his father, Gil, and Coltrane. With his raspy voice and knowing chuckle he said that he would see them all soon enough and that he and Gil and Trane would play some great music again, together.

epilogue

Miles Davis has been dead for almost a decade now and not a day goes by that I don't miss him and his galvanizing presence. Today his five-story-high, black-and-white photographic image is on view on the sides of buildings all across America, in Sony's "Make a Difference" ads. His trumpet and later group sound—as in *Tutu*, *Decoy*, and *Amandla*—are imitated in commercials we hear every day on America's television and radio airwaves. New jazz luminaries such as Cassandra Wilson, Mark Isham, Leo Smith, and many others pay homage to his work. He had an immeasurable influence on my life—and countless others—both as a black man and as an artist. His was a singular spirit, one who marched only to the tempo of his own St. Louis bugle and the rhythms and teachings of his own heart.

Such individuality of spirit can be trying in a country like ours, especially if you are, like Miles Davis, a proud black man who insists on taking risks, doing things his own way, and standing up for his beliefs. Beyond being a risk-taker, Miles was a truly great band leader whose ability to spot great talent launched many distinguished careers. Musicians like Cannonball Adderley, Ron Carter, John Coltrane, Bill Evans, Kenny Garrett, Herbie Hancock, John McLaughlin, Wayne Shorter, Tony Williams, Joe Zawinul, and many others all got their first important exposure working with Miles.

The musical environments that he created for himself and other musicians set up such fertile conditions that everyone who worked inside these innovative scenes flourished. Consider the recording environments he set up for *Kind of Blue, In a Silent Way, Bitches Brew*, and *On the Corner*. By bringing into the recording studio only sketches of what was to be played, Miles forced the musicians to improvise more, to listen more intently to each other, and, further, to respond instantly to the musical flow. Thus, what took place in the studio was the spontaneous sound made in the clubs that musicians love best, where they can improvise and create a coherent collective statement.

Miles was also a great composer and he left us some masterful compositions on *Kind of Blue, On the Corner, Bitches Brew, Filles de Kilimanjaro*, and many other memorable albums. In his own music, he was a voodoo-hoodoo-shaman-man, a witch-doctor-medicine-man-of-roots-music of the highest order. In his most innovative periods, especially after *Kind of Blue*, both his musical theory and his sound were more African than European. He was vilified for this, for moving into a music rooted in group dynamics, such as rock and zouk, rather than staying with Western-oriented jazz, which depends more on individual inspiration and improvisation.

Today, it is a truism that the United States is a multicultural, multiracial country that is home to all kinds of racial, ethnic, cultural, and religious persuasions and institutions. Miles' music reflected all of this diversity before the word "multicultural" was even coined. He listened to and learned from all musical genres. His musical tastes were more than eclectic. They mirrored the changes that were happening in music all over the globe. His last studio recording sessions were for an album that would have included rap. That's why I call him a risk-taker. He was never afraid of failure because failures taught him what he needed to know as much as successes did.

Miles was a great instrumentalist. He had a great melodic, lyrical, and rhythmic approach to playing the trumpet. His beautiful "running" trumpet style has had a lasting impact on younger players. Listening to Miles play, I was always conscious—way before I met him—of being in the presence of a great poet, one who constructed great metaphors through the medium of sound. His sound was very close to that of a human voice. It was a mysterious voice that made me dream. And it wasn't just his tone that was so masterful. Miles' sense of time was phenomenal. Max Roach, the great drummer, said that Miles' "basic quarter note, his time was [always] there: that's why Miles was so profound, because he worked at that." And there was always an edginess about the way he played, a scary intensity and moodiness, something unpredictable. He kept us on our toes.

For at least thirty-five years, Miles Davis was the dominant force in jazz. He just kept listening, playing, and moving toward his own vision. He was an artist whose greatest wish was that he never become, in his own words, "a museum piece under glass." His focus was always on the present and the future, never on the past. In this sense, he was the quintessential American "New World" artist, because he knew that the future is where it is at. He knew that language, technology, instruments—everything that goes into making sound and producing music—changes, and that, to continue to be relevant, music must change, too. He knew that nothing is forever. Everything is forever changing, being torn down or erased to make way for something new. That's just the way it is.

Some critics put down his later music as meaningless or trivial. They say that his many musical changes were driven by commercial reasons rather than artistic ones. But the great majority of music lovers cherished his willingness to go out there on that risky, experimental edge. Ralph Gleason got to the core of this when he wrote: "The greatest single thing about Miles Davis is that he does not stand still. He is forever being born. And like all his other artistic kin, as he changes, leaves behind one style or mode and enters another, he gains new adherents and loses old ones. . . . Miss him at your loss. He is amazing."

He was also amazing as a role model of black pride and

defiance. Miles was what I call an "unreconstructed black man." One who is, to put it simply, someone who doesn't "take shit off no one." Paul Robeson was such a man, as were Malcolm X, Nat Turner, Robert Johnson, Adam Clayton Powell Jr., Huey P. Newton, Stokely Carmichael (later Kwame Toure), and Tupac Shakur, to name just a few who have passed. Unreconstructed black men with us today include Muhammad Ali, Prince, Chuck Berry, Amiri Baraka, and Ishmael Reed.

Unreconstructed black men don't have the manners of their reconstructed "Negro" brethren, who are always trying to put a "civilized" face on their blackness, especially in the company of white folks. Unreconstructed black men will have none of this; they will not play the farcical game they consider beneath them. They get a hard time, therefore, from white people and other "people of color," including black people, many of whom feel threatened by them.

Unreconstructed black men don't submit to power games. "Negro" servants do, and gladly if money is involved. Those "Negro" servants who play along are the ones who get along and receive most, if not all, of the white power structure's patronage. Those who don't play along receive no breaks, and the power structure is always looking for ways to break them. Not because they aren't good Americans, but because they won't kiss ass. Miles Davis refused to play this game and, although he garnered much success in this country, he frequently paid for being an unreconstructed black man.

Unreconstructed black men go their own way and will go to

the mat any time they are challenged. This "unreconstructedness" can cause strange personality quirks that manifest in a highly personalized and self-centered way of looking at and evaluating things. Miles had many of these quirks. Everything in the world revolved around him and the way he looked at it. No compromises: "Either you do it my way or fuck you." I'm not praising this attitude; I'm simply saying that that's the way he was.

In the end, it was very difficult, if not impossible, for Miles ever to see himself as wrong in any situation, because he was focused on what he wanted. That's why he could never say he was wrong, or sorry. Was this a side effect of genius and forty years of success? Of being proven right most times regarding the artistic decisions he made? Maybe. I can't answer that question. What I do know is that it would have been very hard not to be affected by the amount of fame, money, and power Miles acquired over the span of his long career.

Miles had an intuitive grasp of what was right or wrong when it came to blacks, whites, and race relations in this country. This understanding came from the influence of his father—who was a wealthy dentist, a "race man," and one of Miles' biggest supporters—and from his own experiences with racism. Still, ironically, he was deeply insecure about being so dark. Like many dark-skinned blacks he preferred lighter-skinned women to darker ones. "I don't want no woman blacker than me," he used to like to tell me, though it would have been difficult to find such a woman, because there weren't many women darker than he was. It was ironic on another level, too, because many women loved him precisely because of his smooth black skin, and men of all races envied him because of it. The fact that Miles was one of the very first dark-skinned superstar sex symbols in the entertainment industry makes his insecurity over his skin tone even more ironic.

More troublesome was his sexist attitude toward women, which I found deplorable, though I must say here that I never saw him beat or even slap a woman. But his basic attitude was obvious in the language he used when addressing women: "Bitch this" and "Bitch that." His attitude left much to be desired, though in the the last years of his life he found a peaceful serenity and mutual respect in his relationship with Jo Gelbard. I never saw him mistreat her or heard him call or refer to her as a "bitch." Jo seemed to smoothe out his rough edges, and that was good. Maybe she was changing him. I don't know. It appeared so. What I do know is that it was good to see him treat her with the respect that she deserved.

Miles was a sometimes strange, really odd, aloof, seemingly arrogant man, whose contradictions and faults were many, but whose gruff, blunt, even hostile exterior hid from public view a funny and caring person; this was the Miles those who truly knew him loved. I knew all sides of him and I can tell you that his caring and funny side manifested itself in some of his relationships as well as in his art and music.

When we look at the accomplishments of Miles Dewey Davis III over the forty-five-year span of his musical career, we see that he did creative and innovative work in almost all the genres of popular American music—from roadhouse funk all the way to hip-hop. Miles was one of the great artists of the twentieth century, but the music critics and other arbiters of American cultural taste, out of racism and envy, still try to marginalize him, to deny the true measure of his incredible achievement.

Jazz, as a musical genre, is always relegated to the back of the bus in America. People in the music industry, and in the country at large, always say, "It's not commercial enough." But neither is European classical music "commercial enough," and it is hyped and promoted in most big cities. Racism plays an important part in this; European classical music is made and performed mostly by whites for whites. Blacks have been the main innovators and performers during the history of jazz, and, although there have been many white players and fans, it is still thought of as a black art form.

Like that of Malcolm X, Miles Davis' unsmiling, "unreconstructed black" male demeanor remains threatening to many whites and to those middle-class blacks who control institutional largesse outside of the record business—notably at universities, colleges, and Lincoln Center's Jazz Program. In my opinion, this is the chief reason that Miles has been denied his true place in American musical history, in contrast with Louis Armstrong and Duke Ellington, for example, both of whom present that smiling, genial, well-mannered, nonthreatening black male image that is digestible and commercially viable. Institutions like Lincoln Center and colleges and universities mostly rely on grants and the contributions of primarily white benefactors, while record companies rely on sales. Miles Davis has *always* done well at the cash register, and he will continue to do so.

Despite the complexity and narrow audience appeal of European classical music, television programmers do not shy away from promoting it during prime time, in large part because European classical music has its own well-heeled, deep-pocketed advocacy groups, many of whom are positioned in high places in both broadcast and print media. These advocates view promoting this music as protecting and publicizing their own European ancestral roots.

To their credit, the people who run Lincoln Center's Jazz Program view their role with jazz—which they call America's classical music—in the same way. They, too, view themselves as protecting American ancestral roots, but through the promotion of jazz—though it is mostly jazz dating from the mid-1960s on back, what some might call "mainstream" or "straight-ahead" jazz. Avant garde jazz has been, until now, unwelcome here. Yet, with the possible exception of the work of Wynton Marsalis, who plays both American classical and European classical forms of music, even "mainstream" and "straight-ahead" jazz find almost no space on American television airwaves because they don't have the rich and well-positioned advocates in that medium pushing the art form.

Like the music of Mozart and Beethoven, the music of Miles Davis is brilliant, challenging, innovative, fusionistic, and futuristic; it has grandeur and majesty and is orchestral in its sweep. Miles' music should be required listening for all students of

American music in high school, undergraduate, and graduate levels of musical education, but it isn't.

These educational programs are run by academics who have different agendas. Who gets taught often depends on whom the teachers like and who they think is deserving (far too often, their friends). These academics, always suspicious of Miles' technical prowess on the trumpet, often say Miles is unable to play fast and in the higher registers of the instrument. Have they listened to *Four and More, Miles Ahead,* and the many other albums on which he played high and fast after the late 1950s?

Or, citing his many innovations—such as fusing funk, rock, pop, hip-hop, rap, European classicism, and world beat trends with his music, utilizing electrical instrumentation in his own playing and group sound, and removing himself from the "mainstream" purist path—they shun, or at best downplay, his enormous achievements in their classrooms. Similar objections to Miles' unorthodox ways have been made by those, led by Wynton Marsalis, who run the Jazz Program at Lincoln Center.

As we've already seen, it's no secret that the two great trumpeters didn't see "eye to eye" about what constituted great music and even had problems getting along with each other during the last years of Miles' life. At first, during Wynton's first years on the music scene, they got along just fine, with Miles even serving as an early mentor to Wynton before other, more conservative, mentors came along—Stanley Crouch, Albert Murray, and the late Ralph Ellison. Still, these two trumpet titans are fundamentally different in their musical visions. Wynton's vision seems to carry him backward to recover the great jazz—and European classical—music of the past. That's OK. But Miles was steadily trying to move into the future—which is OK also—where jazz has always attempted to go. The fact that their visions clashed is not the problem; the problem is that Wynton has allowed their personal differences to color his judgment of what is or isn't truly great music.

Whatever one's personal musical aesthetic, the fact remains that Miles Davis' impact on and legacy to American and world music are indisputable. Whether Wynton (a great musican and educator in his own right), Stanley Crouch (who detests Miles' music after his second "great quintet" period), Albert Murray, or the late Ralph Ellison personally don't like Miles or his music is not, I repeat, *not,* the point. The point is that his music must be played and memorialized at American institutions because, in the final analysis, Miles Davis has made a great musical contribution to our culture, and it is in the interest of the listening public and future generations of jazz lovers that his aesthetic enemies cast aside their narrow agendas and allow the band of great, young musicians that Wynton has assembled at Lincoln Center to play the music of Miles Davis.

There are still those who will never understand that African Americans don't have to grovel, grin, or kiss white America's collective ass anymore. Those days have long since passed. As we keep trying to move forward as a multicultural country and exploring the ways we see and record our culture and ourselves, I hope that more people will look to Miles Davis as an example of an artist who changed American music in important ways because of his openness to so many musical idioms. Within Miles' flexible, evolving artistic vision, we might find a kind of cultural blueprint that could serve our best interests and point to a more harmonious future. After all, that's what great artists do: they provide us with a perspective that enables us to better understand ourselves and our roles in this rapidly changing world.

Miles Davis has often been justly compared to Pablo Picasso. But most of these comparisons are made in Europe, Latin America, and Japan—not in the United States. Throughout those parts of the world he is revered as a genius who made major contributions to world music and culture. Why not here, in the country of his birth? This question is something that we as a nation are going to have to sort out if we are truly to know ourselves as a people. Perhaps it's the same reason that caused most people in the United States to reject Jimi Hendrix before he was embraced in England, and why Benny Goodman was called the "King of Swing," Paul Whiteman (what an appropriate name!) the "King of Jazz," and Elvis "the King" of whatever. All white men. Today, there are many Americans who hate it when Michael Jackson is called the "King of Pop," because he's black. Well, he *is* the "King of Pop," because nobody else has ever sold as many records in one year as he did *Thriller* or packs more screaming fans into stadiums all over the world. We've got to come to terms with our deep racism and stop pretending that it no longer exists.

What I'm saying is that Miles Davis was just as important to the cultural well-being of the United States as Mozart was to Austria and Picasso to Spain. But the reason that Picasso and Mozart are accepted as true geniuses is that they were white European men and Miles was a black American man. In the end it's alright for Mozart and Picasso to be remembered as arrogant, even imperial, figures. It was part of their birthright to be that way—but it's not supposed to be OK for a black man, not in America. Miles Davis was one our most important cultural barometers despite how we may feel about him as a black person. He represented the best—and worst—of what we are, of our national character (whatever that is), just as Picasso and Mozart represented the very best and worst of their countries' national characters.

Miles Davis was one of the most remarkable creative artists to grace this globe during the entire twentieth century. He changed the course of modern music six or even seven times—an unprecedented feat. For more than forty years, he was our musical Pied Piper, always leading us to the edge of the precipice—the limits of our ability to hear and understand what his music was saying. He led us, sometimes protesting, years into the future. It's uncanny how on the mark he was. Listen to the music of this week's commercials or next year's movie soundtracks. His musical vision is ubiquitous and the sounds that he pioneered are heard everywhere.

Great art has mystery and magic, an attitude, a stance. A reason for being beyond entertainment or decoration, though both of those may also be present. Great artists move the collective spirit by transforming whomever they touch on a deep personal level.

Miles Davis was such an artist and he touched, lived with, and permanently transformed the spirits of many of us.

Miles Davis' music and spirit also live on in the creative expression of the countless musicians, visual artists, dancers, and writers who were influenced by his example and carry forth his vision.

Miles once told me, "When I think about the ones who are dead it makes me so mad, so I try not to think about it. But their spirits are walking around in me, so they're still here and passing it on to others. It's some spiritual shit and part of what I am today is them. It's all in me, the things I learned to do from them. Music is about the spirit and the spiritual, and about feeling. I believe their music is still around somewhere, you know. The shit that we played together has to be somewhere around in the air because we blew it there and that shit was magical, was spiritual."

It is still here with us. We whose lives were changed by Miles can still hear that unforgettable trumpet voice and still feel it going straight into our hearts.

index

illustration credits

Frontispiece. With the author at Miles's apartment, circa 1988: Copyright Jon Stevens.

- With bassist Paul Chambers: Courtesy Euclid Records.
- In his dressing room with Annie Ross, circa 1957: Copyright Lee Tanner / Photography. All rights reserved.
- With Paul Chambers at the Apollo Theatre, 1960: Copyright Herb Snitzer.
- In New York City, circa 1960: Copyright Herb Snitzer.
- At the Jazz Workshop in Boston, circa 1966: Copyright Lee Tanner / Photography. All rights reserved.
- In 1968: Copyright Lee Tanner / Photography. All rights reserved.
- With Dizzy Gillespie: Photo by Frank Stewart.
- At a photo shoot, 1981: Photo by Frank Stewart.
- With Cicely Tyson, 1983: Photo by Risasi Zachariah Dais.
- Clowning with photographer Judy Schiller, 1986: Photo by Judy Schiller.
- In 1990: Copyright William Culhane Jr.
- Jamming with Joseph Foley McCreary: Copyright Herb Snitzer.
- Recording *Kind of Blue*, with (from left) John Coltrane, Cannonball Adderley, and Bill Evans, 1959: Photo by Don Hunstein.
- Same session, with Paul Chambers on bass: Photo by Don Hunstein.

designer: Nola Burger
compositor: Integrated Composition Systems
text: 10.25/16 Electra
display: Univers, Grotesque Extra Condensed
printer and binder: Haddon